Serging for Softies

Black Cats & Overlockers

Jennie Rayment

Acknowledgements

This book is (as ever) dedicated to Nick Diment without whose continually unfailing help, support, advice and encouragement, none of this would ever have happened. He has tolerated tantrums, tears and distress, jollied me along and administered a good kick (metaphorically) when necessary. Marvellous man! He now copes with me in permanent residence and has proof read all the text for this sixth book yet again - he must be mad!

I am very grateful to Patsy Yardley for volunteering to check the proofs. She has worked extremely hard correcting all my multitudinous mistakes and has proffered some invaluable advice. Many thanks are also extended to the indomitable Shelagh Jarvis who was also press-ganged into proof reading.

Pam Neave proved to be a source of wisdom with a multitude of invaluable hints and tips for operating the serger. Plus she was persuaded and cajoled into reading through the text. Enormous thanks have to be extended to Rachael Dorr who did the delectable drawings of the cats. That girl is a real star! One further thank you to Emily Dorr for delving in her graphic files for yet more cat pictures.

A final thank you to Husqvarna Viking (VSM UK Ltd) for lending me a most excellent Huskylock 905; Quilters Treasure (www.QuiltersTreasure.com) for giving me yards of their wonderful marbled fabrics and Lords Sew-Knit Centre (www.lordsewing.co.uk) for their gift of 'Stitch N Shape' made by Floriani.

Copyright © Jennie Rayment 2006   ISBN - 13: 978-0-9524675-7-1
First Published November 2006   ISBN - 10: 0-9524675-7-7
J. R. Publications
5 Queen Street, Emsworth,
Hampshire, PO10 7BJ. England
Tel/Fax: +44 (0)1243 374860
e-mail: jenrayment@aol.com   web site: www.jennierayment.com

Printed by Holbrooks Printers Ltd
Norway Road, Hilsea
Portsmouth, Hampshire PO3 5HX. England
Tel: 02392 661485 Fax: 02392 671119
e-mail: mail@holbrooks.com

International Distributor

USA & World-wide
Quilters' Resource Inc.
3702 Prairie Lake Court,
Aurora, Il 60504, USA
Tel: +630 820 5695 Fax: +630 851 2136
e-mail: info@quiltersresource.com   web site: www.quiltersresource.com

Contents

The cat featured on the front and back cover is Able Seaman Simon:
He was a ship's cat who lived on HMS Amethyst. In April 1949, while the ship was patrolling the China seas, he was badly wounded in a fierce attack. The heavy bombardment maimed and killed many of the crew. Bleeding profusely from deep wounds, Simon was taken to the ship's sick bay along with all the other injured seamen. The little cat, seemingly caring nothing for his own dire state of health, would curl up on the bunks of the sick men. His gentle warmth and soft purring soothed the fevered men and helped greatly in their healing process.

Eventually, months later, the ship docked in Plymouth, where the remaining crew received medals for their bravery under fire. As Simon had been such a source of comfort to the wounded sailors, he also received a medal and was promoted to the rank of Able Seaman.

Sadly, he died in December shortly after the Amethyst docked in England.

Able Seaman Simon

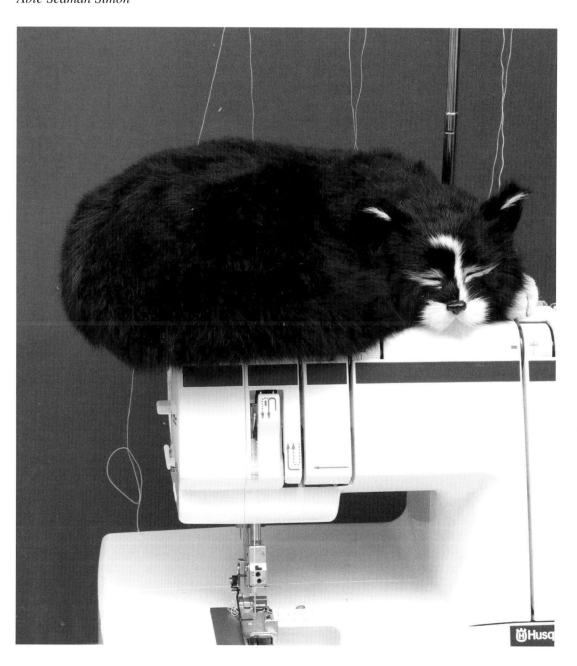

Introduction

Serging for Softies is designed for all sewing aficionados from the very beginner to the more experienced artist. The content is intended to build confidence, create enthusiasm and develop understanding in the use of the serger (overlocker in the UK). A wide variety of very easy projects are offered from Quags to Tucked Totes, with a bit of Weaving for Wussies thrown in for good measure. The projects are simple and suitable for any model of serger from the very basic three-thread to the super-duper top of the range cover stitch machine.

In many workshops, a sad little serger sits, unloved and unused. Get it out, dust it off, thread it up and play. Make friends with the serger, it doesn't bite. The machine sews like mad through nearly everything and is wonderful for creating all manner of different things other than garments. To help the reader, in each chapter, basic settings for the serger are given (minor alterations to the settings may be required for some models).

The text is light-hearted with silly stories and daft ditties to delight and entertain the reader. Each chapter begins with a page of irrelevant burble about my life, the universe and Uncle Tom Cobley and all.

Panic not - if you don't have a serger - make the projects on a sewing machine. The delight of the serger is the speed - 1500 or more stitches a minute, plus it has an amazing ability to cover a raw edge efficiently. Sewing machines can do the same task but are not quite as effective in covering a raw edge and most are not that fast.

Why is this book called Serging for Softies?
This will be obvious when you read the text, as the majority of the creations in this book are soft. (The picky pedants might argue that softish is a better description of some designs.) The original title was 'Black Cats & Overlockers' because of the poem.......

Way down south in the Argentine
A black cat sat on a sewing machine.
The sewing machine went round that fast,
It put six stitches where the cat sat last!

This has to be said fairly carefully ....Now, why has this poem anything to do with sergers or overlockers (call them what you like)? Allow me to recount the tale.

I was sat sitting in my workshop cursing over some serged sample or other when the man came in and stared at what I was doing then said; "It doesn't rhyme!" Mystified, I replied "What doesn't?" "The poem", he said and then repeated the above ditty but substituted 'overlocker' for 'sewing machine'. He was quite right (as ever), it didn't rhyme, but it gave me an idea for a title. A problem immediately arose, most people call this machine a serger and I didn't fancy "Black Cats and Sergers". In addition, would you buy the book if you didn't like cats? Consequently the title was changed to 'Serging for Softies'.

Writing instruction manuals is always hard. Trying to explain simply and in words that everyone could understand is almost impossible at times. I smile when I have read "Lay on a flat surface" and other similar instructions. I can hear the reader querying "Why have I got to do that?" Which reminds me ....Lovely silly joke ....Two elderly people decided that they would get married. Sensibly, they discussed their likes and dislikes beforehand. He delicately raised the subject of sex and wondered how often she might feel the need. Her reply was "In-frequently" and he responded "Is that one word or two?"
PS I was determined to get that somewhere in this book.

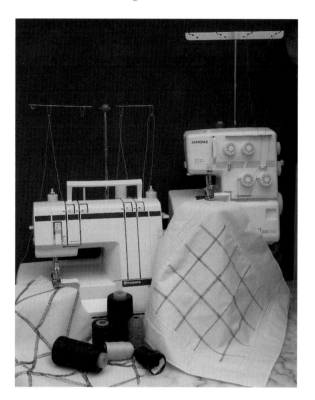

Sergers

Why did I write this book?
I was a sewing machine addict until very recently and had not owned a serger, least of all used one. It had become apparent that many people owned one and rarely used it for any other purpose than covering garment seams. It seemed such a waste (perhaps I should have said - "it seamed such a waist"!). What else would the machine do? Curiosity killed the cat, so I bought a very basic model and played. Shortly afterwards, Husqvarna lent me a mid range model. The projects and ideas in this book are the result of a bit of fiddling, twiddling, nipping and tucking.

Using the sewing machine instead of the serger/overlocker
Follow the same instructions for creating the project

a. Sewing seams
Attach the regular presser foot or the ¼" foot, set stitch length at 2 - 3.

b. Oversewing raw edges
Attach the appliqué foot (check instruction book for the correct one). Set the stitch length at 0.5 - 0.7. Alter the stitch length in fine increments to get the stitching very close. Too large an adjustment (higher number) creates gaps in the stitching; too small an adjustment (lower number) causes the presser foot to jam. (Different threads may need different stitch settings.)

Stitch width is your choice. A wide stitch will give more definition to the edge than a narrow one. Select the width that is suitable for the specific project.

Always run the machine really fast (machine performs more smoothly), guide the work through - no pushing or pulling.

Useful Information

Please read through these next few pages. Most of us skip the 'destructions' only referring to them when disaster looms - nothing works or everything has gone pear-shaped. Advice on the basic operating of the serger (overlocker UK) to the choice of threads plus other useful sewing tips and hints is given in this chapter.

<u>Most Important:</u>
The measurements in the text are given in metric and imperial sizes.
<u>Metric measurements are not always an exact conversion of the imperial ones.</u>
Select either system - do not mix.

Using the serger

Changing the thread and altering the thread tension is a real problem for many people. Panic not - in this book, only simple changes are made to the stitch settings and tensions. In addition, the general purpose presser foot is used for all the projects; no other presser feet are required.

Remember to return the serger settings to normal (as recommended by the manufacturer) at the end of any project and test the stitching. Omit this and the poor old machine gets cursed when you begin the next project because you will have forgotten that you fiddled with the settings. Most stitching problems are operator error and not the machine.

And...........Clean the machine and oil it with the right type of oil. Sunflower, vegetable or engine oil and WD40 are not quite the same as serger/sewing machine oil. Bear in mind - a little lubrication is an excellent thing for all moving parts!

<u>Use the normal standard settings for your serger at all times unless an alteration to these settings is indicated in the text</u>

Where necessary, directions are given in the text for needle position, use of blade, stitch length and width.

Threading

As there are many different models of sergers around today, it is not possible to describe the threading of each and every machine in this book. Nowadays, a DVD or video on the topic is usually supplied when you purchased the machine in addition to the instruction book. Providing you know how to work the video/DVD machine or have a computer then watch the relevant tape or disc. Failing to comprehend these visual aids, read the instruction book carefully. (Sadly the directions in the book are not always written in an understandable format, especially if they have been translated from another language.)

Pleasingly, many sergers are sold ready threaded so you can study the thread system. Some of the more modern models thread automatically, but it is still worth learning how the threading is done because some of the thick decorative embroidery threads won't pass through the automatic system. The machine has to be threaded by hand if this happens.

Prepare the machine

Extend the telescopic stand completely (metal aerial device at the back of machine). Select the thread. Large reels of thread need spool-holders for support or the reels wobble around; small reels require spool caps. Turn the reels so that any notches or other indentations on the spool surface are on the bottom. Ignoring this may cause the thread to snag on the uneven edge of the spool and break - then the machine has to be threaded again.

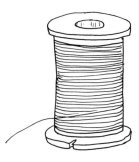

Rules for successful threading

Before you start <u>RAISE</u> the presser foot - DO NOT thread any part of the machine with the presser foot engaged.

Thread from right to left - loopers first then the needles. NO CHEATING.

All the thread guides must be used - do not miss one out. Follow the precise path of any coloured dots or numbers. If the guides are not threaded in the correct sequence, the machine will not sew properly.

Threads must be wrapped round or tucked under any tension discs properly. A sharp tug may be needed to get the thread to lie securely within the tension disc.

Threading the loopers

Open the front of the machine and look at the thread system. Coloured marks indicate the path of the thread to each of the loopers. Arm yourself with a pair of tweezers and a needle-threader: these are ideal tools for grabbing or feeding the thread through awkward places. Draw a deep breath and begin. Don't be frightened - it is only a serger not a life-threatening piece of equipment. Lying down in a darkened room will not get the machine threaded.

Thread the lower looper

This can be awkward to thread. Take the extreme right-hand thread and follow the coloured pathway indicated for the lower looper. Many models have a small lever to push or pull before you can access the lower looper eye; other models have to have the free arm cover removed or pulled aside beforehand. If necessary use tweezers and a needle-threader to get the thread through the eye of the lower looper. Pull about 10 cm (**4"**) of thread through on completion and leave it lying on the right of the presser foot. (Chocolate soothes frazzled nerves.)

Thread the upper looper

Take the next thread (second from right). Follow the coloured pathway exactly. Make sure that the thread passes through that little eye on the upper looper. Use the tweezers or a needle-threader to pass the thread through the eye (essential if you have selected bulk (woolly) nylon thread). Once the threading is complete pull about 10 cm (**4"**) of thread through and leave it lying on the right-hand side of the presser foot.

Thread the needles

This is an easy operation compared to threading the loopers. Remember to keep the presser foot raised before starting to thread the needles. Follow the coloured markings, taking care to get the thread slotted into or round the tension discs. Pull 10 cm **(4")** of thread through afterwards.

Tip: Instead of removing a reel when changing from a four thread overlock stitch to three threads, cut the thread immediately above the needle, leaving it slotted through the tension disc. Tape the loose thread end to the body of the machine (masking tape is ideal) to prevent it catching in another part of the mechanism.

Now remember to breathe! Place the all the threads under the presser foot. Test the stitching - hopefully all is well.

BUT BUT BUT......... Why not cheat?

Who says that you have to keep re-threading the machine? Why not tie a new thread to the original one and pull it through the system? This is very useful in threading the loopers but I find it just as quick to rethread the needles from the beginning rather than fiddle around tying knots.

Cut the looper and the needle threads just above the spool. Tie the new threads <u>firmly</u> to the original ones, use a reef/square knot (granny knots tend to come undone). Trim the ends.

The threads can be pulled through the system in two ways:

a. Run the machine slowly until the new threads are through. Pull the chain gently as you sew. Ease the knots through the tension discs. If the knot will not pass through the needle, cut the thread when the knot is level with the needle and thread the needle as normal. (It may be necessary to slacken the tensions - turn dials to a lower number.)

b. Turn the hand-wheel clockwise (away from you); this will release the thread chain allowing you to pull the new threads through the system by hand - no need to sew. Pull the original threads through the system. Amazingly the new threads will come through providing you tied proper knots. Pull the thread gently as the knots pass through the tension discs and the looper eyes. If the knot will not pass through the needle, cut the thread when the knot is level with the needle and thread the needle as normal.

Now test the stitching.

If the machine makes a very strange noise - a reel of thread is probably caught on the telescopic stand or has fallen off the spool pin and the cat has it.

One last word of advice ....

SHOULD THE LOWER LOOPER THREAD BREAK - REMOVE THE THREAD FROM THE NEEDLES FIRST. THREAD THE LOWER LOOPER THEN RETHREAD THE NEEDLES.

<u>IF YOU DON'T DO THIS THE MACHINE WILL NOT SEW</u>

Choice of thread

Most machine threads made from polyester, cotton and rayon to many of decorative metallic ones are suitable for the serger. As the loopers consume vast quantities of thread, the large reels (5000 yards/metres or more) are more economical than small ones. Many of the projects in this book are sewn with bulk (woolly) nylon. This is a thick fluffy thread that expands slightly when sewn. It provides an excellent coverage over a raw edge. <u>Bulk nylon is used on the loopers only</u>. It is too coarse to thread through the eye of the needle unless..................... I digress................

The chairman (head honcho) of a very eminent overlocker company in the UK decided to mend his daughter's sports shorts one evening. He took a brand new machine home with several reels of bulk nylon - a simple job he assured his daughter - it would take only a moment. All he had to do was sew one small seam. Hours later, cursing and swearing, he nearly threw the machine in the bin. Trying to get the bulk nylon through the needle proved extremely difficult, and when he did achieve it the thread broke and the needle had to be re-threaded once again. It became an absolute nightmare made worse by his daughter repeatedly asking "Daddy, haven't you finished it yet?" Eventually, he managed to complete the seam albeit in a rough and ready fashion.

Moral of this story is REMEMBER that bulk nylon is <u>not</u> threaded through the needles, only through the loopers, and if you are the chairman of a prestigious company - either learn how to use the product or keep quiet about your incompetence. This chap is a lovely guy and he doesn't deserve the flack he has had since relating this sorry tale.

Now to continue........Have no qualms about using tweezers or a needle-threader to thread bulk nylon through the looper eyes. (Slot the needle-threader through the looper from the back - insert the bulk nylon and pull the needle-threader back through the looper).

For decorative glossy finishes, try floss. This is a shiny slippery thread, which usually needs a sleeve over the spool to stop the thread sliding off. Lacking a sleeve, try.......

Tip: *Remove the reel from the spool pin. Place it in a narrow glass or small high-sided pot. Set the glass/pot on the table at the back of the machine (under the telescopic bar).*

Why not mix those wonderful variegated machine and fancy metallic threads for an unusual finish? Test the stitching in case the tensions have to be adjusted. Bulk nylon and other thick threads usually require a reduced tension (turn tension dial to a lower number). Fine slippery threads need to have a tighter tension (turn dial to a higher number).

Breaking threads?
Reduce the tension (turn dial to lower number) on the relevant disc, allowing the thread to run through more freely. Alternatively, insert a new needle - the old one may be blunt.

Ironing over stitching
Some of the decorative threads melt when pressed - always use a cloth or pressing sheet over the seam. Prevention is better than a singed and shrivelled mess.

Finally: Three thread overlock or four? That is the question.

In my opinion, a three thread overlock looks more attractive on an exterior seam than a four thread one. In addition, a three thread overlock uses less yarn than a four thread; there is only one needle eye to struggle with and only three not four tension discs to adjust. The choice is yours.

Setting the tensions

Before you begin to fiddle with the dials make a note of the original settings recommended by the manufacturer (usually indicated somewhere in the instruction book). Should the stitching go totally awry after you have twiddled the tension discs then reset to the original settings. Hopefully the machine will now sew properly again. (Might need more chocolate or quick stroke of the cat.)

The most important rule with the tension is to increase or decrease the settings on the dials <u>slightly</u>, one dial at a time, and keep testing the stitching.

Looper threads should meet evenly on the edge of the fabric. The <u>upper looper</u> is the thread on the <u>top</u> side of the material, the <u>lower looper</u> on the <u>bottom</u>. Magic!

Needle threads should lie flat and not pucker. If you are uncertain about the quality of the stitching, open the seam and pull. The stitching should be firm.

The instruction book will tell you how to adjust the tension but make time one day to experiment. **<u>Thread the machine with different colours on each spool</u>** - much easier to identify the individual threads. Try altering the tensions and look at the stitching. See what happens when you turn the tension dials up or down. Sit and play - it is well worth it.

Before you alter any tension, check that the threads are feeding through properly. A thread may have caught on the spool causing the problem and there may be nothing wrong with the tensions.

To **loosen** the tension turn dial to a **LOWER** number.
To **tighten** the tension turn dial to a **HIGHER** number.

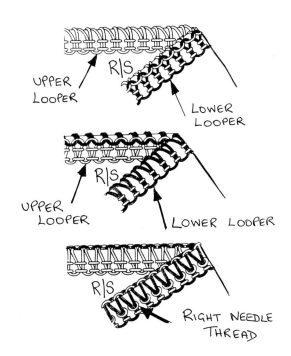

<u>Upper looper thread shows on the underside of the seam</u>: Tighten the tension (higher number) on the dial or reduce the tension (lower number on the lower looper). Try one option at a time.

<u>Lower looper thread shows on the top side of the seam</u>: Tighten the tension on the lower looper dial (higher number) or reduce the tension on the upper looper (lower number). Try one option at a time.

<u>Right or left-hand needle thread loops on the underside</u> - tighten the tension (higher number).

<u>Curling fabric edge -</u> loosen tension on both loopers.

<u>Puckering fabric</u> - loosen one or both needle threads.

Altering the stitch length and width may affect the tension.

Changing stitch length

The stitch length is the distance along the seam of one stitch. Turning the dial/lever towards a higher number from the recommended standard increases the length of the stitch. Turning the dial/lever to a lower number decreases the stitch length.

Increasing the stitch length may require the tensions on the thread to be loosened. A decreased stitch length may need the tension to be tightened. Why? .... The tension discs affect the speed at which the thread runs through.

Less tension = more thread - More tension = less thread

Loosening the tension allows the thread to run through faster, tightening slows the speed of the thread. Longer stitches take more thread; smaller stitches need less thread. More thread is required for longer stitches and less thread for shorter stitches.

Changing stitch width

The stitch width is the distance across the seam of one stitch. Unlike sewing machines, the stitch width on a serger can be altered in several ways:

a. Adjust the distance between the blade (knife) and the needles. The distance between the blade and the needle is often called the 'bite'. Setting the blade nearer to the needles decreases the stitch width, setting the blade further from the needles increases the stitch width.

b. Change the number of needles.

c. Retract or extend the stitch finger* (see instruction manual). A lever or sliding knob/button usually operates the stitch finger; pull it back to reduce the width, push it forwards to increase.

> *__Not all machines have a single stitch finger operated by a lever or sliding knob, on some models the stitch finger is altered by changing the needle plate. Read the instruction manual to see if the machine has a stitch finger (not applicable to all models) and if so - how is it operated?.__

Reduce the stitch width - without altering position of the blade
Remove the left-hand needle. For a further reduction, retract the stitch finger as far as possible from the needle. Alternatively change the needle plate. (See above.)

Increase the stitch width - without altering position of the blade
Insert left-hand needle. Extend the stitch finger. The further the stitch finger is extended the wider the stitch width. Alternatively change the needle plate. (See above.)

As discussed in the section on stitch length, a wide stitch width may need the tension loosening, a narrow stitch width, tighter tension. Why? More thread is required for wider stitches and less thread for narrower ones.

Setting a 0.65 cm (¼") seam
Remove the left-hand needle. Retract the stitch finger as far as possible or change the needle plate for the smaller size. Set the edge of the presser foot on the raw edge of the fabric. The distance between the raw edge of the fabric and the right-hand needle should measure 0.65 cm (¼"). Check this as models vary.

Using the blade/upper cutter

For many of the projects in this book, the blade (sometimes called the upper cutter) is used solely for removing the whiskers of thread from the edge of the fabric not for trimming the material. Watch the blade carefully as it runs along the edge of the material - do not gouge great lumps out of the fabric.

Seeing the edge of the blade is awkward when the machine is flat on the table. Tilting the machine offers a clearer view of this area. Think about it. You tilt your book to read, tilt the computer keyboard, an artist tilts the easel and yet you hunch over the flat bed of the serger.

Tip: Purchase two rubber doorstops and place them under the base of the machine at the back. Tilt the machine towards you.

Rubber doorstops, barbecue skewers, flower pins, and Tak gun.

Finishing off the seam

Seams can be secured by hand or on the machine.

There are several recommended ways to hand finish a seam:
For all three methods, chain off the end of the seam leaving approximately 10 cm (**4"**) of thread. (For those who are new to sergers, 'chaining off' is a serger term for 'continue sewing off the fabric leaving a trail of threads'.)

a. Unravel the chain stitching and tie the thread ends together.
b. Use a crochet or rouleau hook to pull the chain through the stitching.
c. Thread the ends into a needle and sew them through the line of machine stitching. A needle with an open-ended eye (Easy Threader) is a handy gadget here.

By machine:
Sew one stitch past the end of the seam. Turn the work round and flip it over. Sew back over the previous stitches for about 2 cm (**1"**), chain off and cut the threads flush with the seam.
Do not cut the original stitching with the blade.

Alternatively, cut the threads flush with the seam end. Apply some type of seam sealant like Fray Check or fabric glue and stick the threads down. (See photograph)

Personally, I prefer to glue the ends together or thread the ends back into the seam with a needle. On odd occasions I have used whatever adhesive I can find to stop the stitches unravelling, including the hot melt glue gun. Word of warning - select your adhesive carefully if the item is to be washed or given to small children.

Sewing round a corner

For this information, I have to thank Pam Neave, the head of education for Viking Sewing Machines in the UK. Her helpful hints, advice and splendid notes were most appreciated.

Important: Trim any excess fabric to the seam allowance <u>before</u> sewing round any inner or outer corner. Use scissors or a rotary cutter.

<u>Outer corners</u>: This technique works with all materials.

1. Stop sewing at edge of the corner. Sew one stitch beyond the edge of the fabric and raise presser foot.

2. Lift the needle to its highest position. Rotate the hand wheel towards you (anti-clockwise).

3. Slip your finger under the needle threads. Pull the threads through gently to form a loose loop.

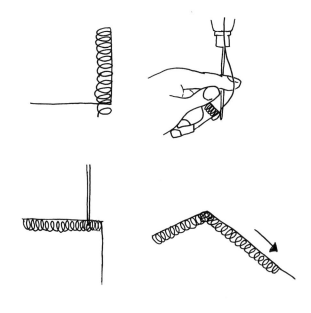

4. Turn the fabric (it might need a little jiggle to turn freely). Check that the stitches are released from the stitch finger. Insert the needle into the sewn edge of the fabric at the same seam allowance as before. Lower the presser foot and sew to next corner or end of seam.

Tip: Sewing squares: Follow the above technique for three corners, on the last corner, chain off and secure the threads (page 13).

<u>**Inner Corners**</u> *(Technique not applicable to owners of cover stitch machines)*
Only fabrics that can be pleated or folded easily can be used. This technique is not suitable for any stiff or rigid materials. In addition, the finished corner will be slightly rounded - not a perfect right-angle. Does it matter?

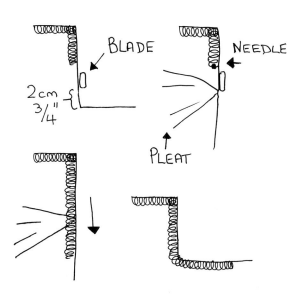

1. Sew the seam until blade is approximately 2cm (¾") from the corner. **STOP**. <u>DO NOT</u> cut the fabric.

2. Drop the needle/s into the fabric. Raise the presser foot. Straighten the corner by pulling the material. Pull firmly - a 'V' shaped pleat will form.

3. Realign the edge of the material with the edge of the presser foot. This might require jiggle (of the fabric not you!).

4. Lower the presser foot and sew to the end of the seam.

Flatlock seam

As the name describes, the seam can be pulled completely flat. On one side of the fabric the stitching resembles a ladder, on the other side it is similar to the regular serger seam. Both sides of the stitch pattern can be used for embellishment and decoration. (The needle thread only shows on the ladder side of the seam.) In addition, a flatlock seam is ideal for attaching lace, ribbons and braids to the edge of the fabric.

1. Remove the right-hand needle and disengage the blade.

2. Loosen left-hand needle tension - turn to lower number.

3. Tighten lower looper tension to higher number.

4. Stitch width variable:
Narrow flatlock - retract stitch finger. Wide flatlock - extend stitch finger.

The side of the presser foot is aligned with the edge of the fabric - try not to deviate.

On completion of any flatlock seam, pull the seam firmly with one hand on either side of the material - give it a bit of welly (UK term meaning to put effort in). Press flat.

Rolled Hem seam

A most excellent way to finish a raw edge with a narrow hem. For a really good coverage of the raw edge, use bulk nylon or any other thick decorative thread. Most machines do not require the presser foot to be changed, but check the instruction book in case your particular model requires a different presser foot and/or needle plate (see instruction book).

1. Remove the left-hand needle. Keep the blade engaged.

2. Tighten the lower looper tension - set at a higher number (refer to manual).

3. Set the stitch length at the size recommended for the chosen project.

Use a waste catcher

Attach a little bag or tray to the front of the machine to catch thread and fabric trimmings or get a good vacuum cleaner!

Don't forget to clean and oil the machine regularly: regularly does not mean once in a blue moon!

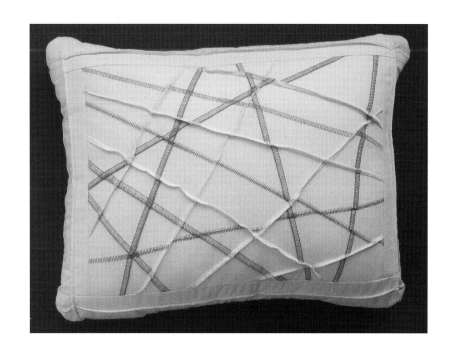

Flatlock seams.
Jennie Rayment

More helpful hints

The following section has odd snippets of information in no particular order of importance.

Choice of materials

Most types of fabrics can be used for the projects in this book, but crisply finished materials with a firm weave are easier to handle than loosely woven limp ones. Crisp materials also hold their shape as opposed to flaccid floppy fabrics.

Medium-weight cottons, chintzes (glazed cotton), cretonnes and indeed calico (known as muslin in USA) or silk are ideal. Softer fibres (wool, voiles, and gauze) and finely woven fabrics (thin silks and lawns) do not support texture well, but are excellent if you desire a less defined effect. Thick materials such as velvets, corduroys, tweeds, felt and heavy linens are often too rigid to twist into intricate patterns, although by enlarging the selected textured design the result can be most effective.

Frequently, polyesters and other man-made fibres are too crease resistant to hold any textured effect efficiently. Needless to say, some of the modern micro-pore fabrics look superb when textured and embellished.

Colour and pattern selection

Plain and pale coloured materials display a textured surface clearly and have good light reflecting qualities. Chintz and lustrous silk respond well to texture: their inherent shine adds depth to the light and shade cast by the textured areas. Hand-dyed materials and very fine self-coloured prints are also a good choice. Darker and heavily patterned fabrics absorb more light and may conceal the finer details of an elaborate tucked or textured design. Oddly enough black chintz is most effective, although the light source has to be correct for the full textural effects to be apparent. Use of different colours or tints, tones and shades of the same hue will enhance the dynamics of the design (great phrase!).

Washing fabrics

Many people recommend pre-washing of the fabric to prevent further shrinkage of the finished project or any problems with dye colours running. This is an unmitigated nuisance but sensible. Use of a "colour catcher" (readily obtainable in supermarkets) is advisable when washing dark or strong colours. (These are small paper-like sheets treated with a special ingredient that prevents individual dye colours contaminating other colours.)

Wash the fabric in cool water (the creases won't set so easily), then tumble dry or line dry until damp. Press it well with either a steam or dry iron (depends on the amount of creasing). Spray starch to restore the 'body'. (Starch the material before cutting, as the heat of the iron and the moisture from the starch may stretch and distort the pieces.)

Fusing fabrics

Several of the ideas in this book need stiffening with a heavyweight interfacing. Fabric is fused (glued) to one or both sides of the interfacing at the start of the project. These days, there are several products available in many craft/sewing stores, which are ideal for the projects because they have a fusible surface on both sides. Two of these are:

a. Fast2fuse (C & T Publishing - www.ctpub.com). Obtainable in regular or heavy weight.

b. Stitch N Shape (Floriani - www.floriani.com). Can be steamed into shape if crushed.

BUT....... Not everyone has access to these fusible products so make your own:

Purchase a heavy craft-weight interfacing and one of the fusible glue webs such as Bondaweb, Trans Web or Wundaweb or other similar product. Fuse the glue web to the fabric <u>first</u> then fuse the fabric to the interfacing. (Fusing the glue web directly onto both sides of the interfacing may result in the interfacing becoming adhered to the ironing board cover - I tried!)

Tips for successful fusing
a. Read the instructions - the heat temperature varies according to the product.

b. Always use a pressing sheet (*Teflon coated pressing sheets available from June Tailor - www.junetailor.com.*), waxed paper, silicone baking sheets (from the supermarket) or some other protective layer between the iron and the fusing product in addition to one between the fabric and the ironing board cover. If glue gets on the ironing board cover it sticks to everything else.

Glue on material
Wait until the fabric has completely cooled. Hold the fabric firm and scrape the marks off very gently using an edge of a sharp blade. Shave the surface of the material only - mind your fingers.

Glue on iron
Although there are several products available for removing glue from the sole plate, a metal pot-scourer is also effective. If you can find them, the round pot-scourers constructed from a mesh of fine metal strands are the best. **DO NOT** use this on any iron with a Teflon coated sole plate.

Heat the iron to maximum. Place the metal scourer under the sole plate and rub the iron firmly across the mesh. Sometimes wetting the scourer makes it work more efficiently.

Scorch marks
Remove these with lemon juice or a weak solution of hydrogen peroxide (stuff used for lightening hair). Use a dry cloth and rub firmly. Unwashed cloth scorches more easily than washed as the dressing singes quite quickly.

Thread Saver
Don't yawn, I know this tip has been in all my books because it really does save yards of thread. Thread is expensive - try this technique on the serger. It is a most useful natty notion and saves reels of thread. It is not my own idea - it's an old tailoring trick.

A thread saver enables <u>continuous sewing</u>, rather like chain piecing in patchwork.

Rummage in the trash bin and find a small scrap of unwanted fabric. At the end of any line of stitching **<u>DO NOT</u> lift the presser foot, <u>DO NOT</u> remove the work or cut the threads,** but continue to sew. **<u>Chain off the work on to this scrap of material and STOP on the scrap</u>**. The presser foot is now sitting on the scrap of material. Leave the scrap there - do not move it.

Detach the work from the small scrap by cutting the threads immediately behind (at the back of) the presser foot (between scrap and work).

Continue with the next set of seams. Sew off the scrap and down the next seam (scrap is now attached to the start of the work). At the end of this line of stitching, cut the scrap off from the start and sew from the main piece of work on to the scrap once again. Cut threads behind the presser foot. Repeat, repeat, repeat etc.!

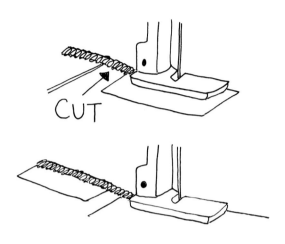

This scrap is called a thread saver and will save a vast amount of thread - no long dangling chains of stitch; And and and…..For those who habitually deviate at the end of a seam, it may keep you on the straight and narrow - try it. It may help.

Give the idea a whirl - it seems complicated but is very easy when you get the hang of it. The scraps of fabric can always be kept and stitched together - just think of the amazing wall-hanging you could create from these little bits! But life is too short....

Remember: the only place to cut the threads is <u>behind the presser foot</u> (once you have sewn on to the thread saver and have <u>stopped</u>).

Pinning fabric

NEVER put any pin where it can possibly get caught under the serger presser foot whilst you sew along the seam. ALWAYS put pins at right-angles to the fabric edge, and remove them before you sew past. Sewing over a pin ruins the cutting blade and doesn't do the pin any good!

Flower pins are my favourite choice of pin because they are extremely sharp, long and have a flat head (photograph page 13). They pass easily through many layers and, when ruling or cutting, the heads lie happily under a ruler. BUT the flower ends tend to fall off leaving a fairly useless pin. It is also possible to sew through the pin heads. Overall the pros outweigh the cons in my opinion, so treat yourself to some. Just be careful to buy the right sort as one type of these pins is not as fine or sharp, more like a poker. Ask before you purchase.

Wooden barbecue sticks (Photograph page 13)

These are an absolute must. They are ideal for holding the layers together when feeding them under the presser foot; pushing recalcitrant corners under whilst stitching; poking points out (use the blunt end), and scoring guidelines on material. These can be obtained from most hardware/ironmongers stores and many supermarkets. Barbecue sticks are available in a variety of sizes. The best size is 15 cm (**6"**) as the much longer 25 cm (**10"**) ones are a little unwieldy, but you can snap the end off to reduce the size. I have always found anything 15 cm (**6"**) long to fit very comfortably in my hand, much to the delight of my man!

UK English versus US English

It is not the same!

Calico

UK: Pure unbleached cotton cloth of varying weights from a very fine weave to one suitable for upholstery.
US: Light to medium weight cotton fabric, often printed with a small floral design, and used for making patchwork and children's dresses.

Muslin

UK: Pure cotton cloth with a very open weave - sometimes used for straining foodstuffs.
US: Pure unbleached cotton cloth of varying weights from a very fine weave to one suitable for upholstery (exactly the same as UK calico).

Tacking/basting

In Britain, tacking refers to a long stitch length. In the US, it means to stitch/secure firmly on the spot.

Cross Grain

In the UK, this is any cut on the bias/diagonal, but in the US it is a cut across the material from selvedge to selvedge.

Finally, when you have made all the projects and conquered the serger, upgrade the machine to a cover stitch model. This combines the most of the attributes of a serger with the some of the versatility of a sewing machine. This machine will sew in the middle of the fabric as well as on the edge. Watch this space - maybe I will get one and write a seventh book.

Wiggly Weaving samples embellished with chain and triple cover stitches. Sewn on Huskylock 936 using clear presser foot. (www.husqvarnaviking.com) Pam Neave

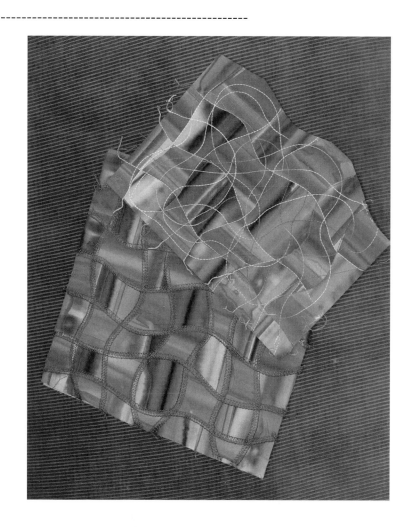

Big Sling Bag

Star-spangled bangles

Sat sitting at the computer, it is remarkably easy for one's fingers to wander erratically over the keyboard and transpose the letters. Not long ago, I was slightly appalled to reread an email where I had warmly invited someone to bring her 'fiend' to the class. Frequently Guild secretaries have received a note from me assuring them that their booking was in the dairy rather than in the diary. I felt a little better when I received a letter from a secretary referring to the 'Quitters Guild'. Still it was a little odd to be asked to lecture to a Townswomen's Guild for 45 minuets. Would I get Chopined off if I overran?

There have been several other rather silly typing errors in my past that I deeply regret. (Why does 'f' come next to 'd' on the keyboard?) As a young trainee in a big London hotel typing 'Roast _uck and orange sauce' on the restaurant menu did not earn me many brownie points! The dish sold well! As did the 'Smoked Tout'. It is much more better to read what is writ before hitting the print button.

Typing errors are minor compared to some other major whatsit-ups I have made in life. One memorable incident involves the man!

It was early days in our relationship - those starry-eyed beginnings when the heart pounded, the knees knocked, the breathing was constricted, the wondering.......would he, wouldn't he .....? What a joy those fledgling instances of undying passion were. (I am going to write a bonk-buster next!!)

Anyway............ He arrived in <u>my car</u> (he is not daft - I pay for the fuel) at Heathrow to collect me from some international trip or other. Once the moment of passionate greeting was over, I flumped into the car.

"Any sweeties, please?" (I always need a sugar hit after a long flight.)
"Yes", he replied "In the glove compartment."

I opened it. Nestled in a nest of Werthers (gold wrapped sweets) was a superb gold bangle. Instantly, I seized it saying very peremptorily, "Who have YOU had in my car?" (Thinking to myself, "How dare he have another woman in my car. I pay for the fuel!")

How was I (jet-lagged and bemused) to know that this was a highly romantic gesture? The bangle was a gift for me, a symbol of his love and affection. Ahhhhhh!

Twelve years later, I still have the bangle and the same man. I suspect he should be given a medal, as he has just become longest serving man in my life. None of the other men in my life have put up with me for so long. Can't think why!

Big sling bag

Take this bag to the shops, to the beach, on holiday, on every excursion and expedition or wherever you fancy. It can be carried or slung over the shoulder and will hold absolutely everything. It is most excellent for taking on holiday as it folds into a small package and slots easily in that last remaining corner of your overstuffed suitcase. As an added bonus, the big sling bag is reversible. Combine two colour schemes, one for the inside and one for the outside then turn the bag to suit your ensemble of the day.

Measurements are given in this chapter for a specific size but the big sling bag can be made from any four equal-sized rectangles. The length (longest side) of the rectangle should be at least twice the width (shortest side): Long narrow rectangles make deep bags with a small base, short wide rectangles make shallow sided bags with a large base.

Material choice
For really big bags, furnishing fabrics are ideal, smaller bags can be made from lighter-weight materials. Washable, easy-care materials are ideal.

As the bag is reversible, why not construct one side of the bag in two contrasting fabrics. and choose two differently coloured fabrics for the inside?

Thread selection
Bulk nylon on both loopers and standard polyester through the needles is a good combination of threads. Choose a colour that compliments or contrasts with the material.

Big Sling Bag:
Fabrics by Jan Mullen
(Stargazey Quilts
www.stargazey.com)

Jennie Rayment

For a multicoloured reversible sling bag: you need
Four 25 x 112/115 cm **(9 x 44/45")** strips of fabric in four different colours
Or Four *'fat quarters' in four different colours
(*A 'fat quarter' is a half metre/yard of material cut midway between the selvedges
creating two pieces approximately 50 x 112/115 cm **(18 x 22")** wide.)

1. Cut:
Bag: Eight 20 x 50 cm **(8 x 20")** rectangles (two rectangles from each colour)
Handles: Four 4.5 x 48 cm **(1¾ x 19")** strips (increase or decrease length to suit)

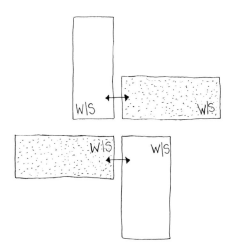

Serger Settings: Regular
*(Select three/four thread overlock (see page 10).
Seam allowance is irrelevant - be consistent.)*

2. Take four rectangles (use two different fabrics).
Lay the pieces on a flat surface alternating the
colours. Sew two rectangles together. (Watch the
cutting blade - it should be trimming the whiskers
not carving lumps from the fabric edge!) Repeat
with the other two.

3. Sew both sets
together to form a
cross, turning each
seam in the
opposite direction.
Press carefully.

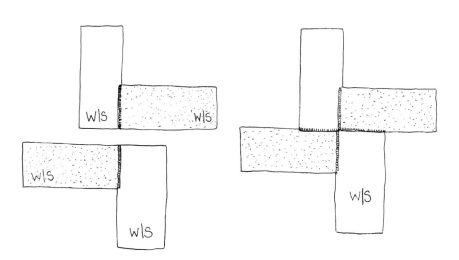

4. Join the remaining four rectangles
together in a **mirror image** of Stage 1
and 2.

*Tip: Lay the first side of the bag R/S
up on a flat surface. Place the
remaining four sections R/S down
on top. Sew together in that order.
Check each stage - it is extremely
easy to get things very wrong!*

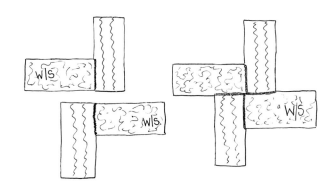

5. Take one of the stitched sections. This next instruction seems strange, but trust me and try it!

Fold point **A** over to touch point **X (see diagram)**. Align the raw edges. Sew from the centre outwards. Repeat on the other three points bringing **B** to **Y**, **C** to **Z** and **D** to **W**.

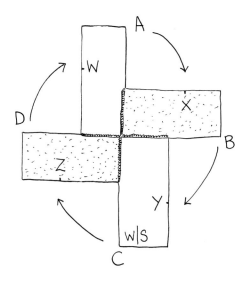

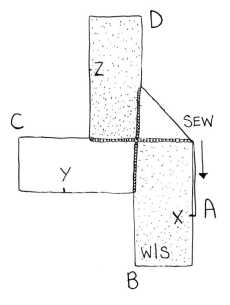

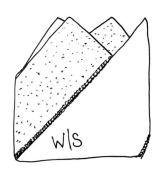

6. Rest this slightly strange shape on a flat surface. Wriggle it a bit to form a square based bag with four points at the top (W/S out).

7. Repeat the last two stages with the other cross-shaped section. Turn **right side out**. Wriggle it into a square based bag as described above. Drop the first section inside this one.

8. Align the raw edges and pin both sections together.

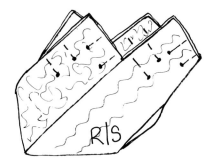

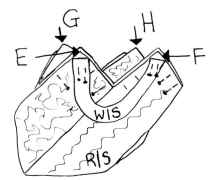

9. Pin one 4.5 x 48 cm (**1¾ x 19"**) handle strip to the <u>outer fabric</u> at points **E** and **F** (both fabrics R/Ss together). <u>Do not pin the handle to the inner fabric</u>. Repeat with another handle strip on the other two points of the bag (**G** and **H**). <u>Do not twist the strips</u>.

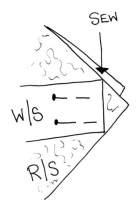

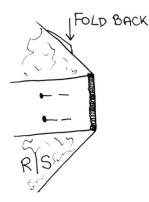

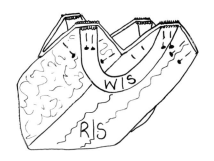

10. Sew the handles to the outer side of the bag only.

Tip: Pin the inside section of the bag away from the stitching.

11. Pin the remaining two handle strips to the inside of the bag and sew in place.

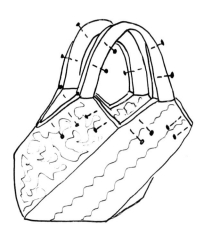

12. Pin both sides of both handles together.

13. Sew both sections of the bag together. Start the stitching sewing near one of the seams. Sew round raw sides of the bag and round the handle.

Keep the raw edge level - pull any angled junctions straight (page 14). Take great care to prevent the blade from cutting the fabric. On completion, raise the needles and pull the work out. Chain off and tidy the threads afterwards.

14. Sew round the remaining raw edges of the bag and the handles in the same fashion.

Give the bag a quick press. Decide which fabric will be on the outside, turn to suit. Grab your purse/handbag, credit card or check/cheque book and go shopping!

Why not make another bag from other fabrics? For a bigger or smaller sling bag just change the sizes of the rectangles.

Larger rectangles = bigger bag = more shopping!

Crazy Log Cabin

The more I travel the more I become aware that the English spoken in the USA is not the same as the English in the UK. These days, I am used to elevator/lift, faucet/tap, bonnet/hood, trunk/boot, fender/bumper, purse/handbag, restroom/lavatory to name but a very few (see page 19). The British use a hoover to clean the carpet but the Americans have a vacuum. Humping in the UK is 'carrying' - it has a slightly different meaning in the US. Sometimes I just don't understand ....

Erica's basket

Some months ago I was staying with a good American friend of mine who runs a sewing store in South Bend, Indiana. For one reason or another, I had a day free but she had to work. I was left in the house to amuse myself. A day off in a house with an enormous sewing room crammed with fabric, threads and sewing machines - a sewer's delight! Guess what I was going to do. Erica had asked me to make certain that all thread ends and scraps of material were put in the covered basket in case her highly cherished cats consumed them. If the cats ate the threads they would suffer the most appalling digestive problems. It did not bear thinking about, especially as the cats lived indoors!

I sewed all day, diligently putting every thread, scrap or bit in a pretty lined wicker basket with a frilly decorative lid that lay under the sewing table. It was the only basket I could see. It seemed a slightly odd repository for the rubbish but it was a <u>basket</u> and I was in a foreign country - people do things differently. (There was nothing else in the basket so it must have been recently emptied, or so I thought.)

A day later, I returned to the UK. On the way to the airport Erica commented on how little sewing I had done on my day off. She had gone to empty the basket and it was empty! Panic struck - had the cats eaten all those threads?

Thank goodness I was going home, just think of the mess. I kept very quiet. She chatted on and asked if I had noticed the fabric lined bassinet with the frilly lid, which she had delivered to a special customer that morning. I did not know that in the corner of her workshop was a lidded plastic <u>waste bin</u>, which Erica always referred to as a 'basket'!

I wonder what the customer thought when she lifted the lid of her basket and saw all the threads and scraps of rubbish in the bottom.

Crazy Log Cabin

Quick and easy to prepare, fast and simple to sew, this technique is ideal for all. The design is based on a traditional form of patchwork known as Log Cabin (sometimes called Log Wood in Canada). It is an extremely popular pattern among most patchwork bods and I suspect nearly all of them have made some form of Log Cabin cushion or quilt. Many books covering the different construction methods, pattern arrangements and the history of the design have been written. Research the local library, quilt store or surf the Internet for further information on this fascinating topic.

Log cabin cushion: Jennie Rayment

In the standard Log Cabin design, a centre square is bordered with strips - one strip on each side. In Crazy Log Cabin, strips are added at a slight angle to the edge of the central shape - the angle can be subtly different each time. This produces a series of blocks with a randomly distorted design.

Unlike many sewing projects, this particular technique is ideally suited to the serger or overlocker (call it what you will). The primary function of the machine is to cut as it sews as it goes - exactly what is required. If the sewing machine is used, time is lost with trimming the excess material after each seam.

Crazy Log Cabin is template free so there are no worries about cutting exact shapes and sizes or sewing a precise seam allowance. Just cut a square-ish chunk of material and add some strips; sew a few seams and square off the result. It's a doddle to do, so have a go!

Fabric choice

Crazy Log Cabin can be created from a wide variety of materials from velvets to voiles. For preference, firmly woven pure cotton materials in plain colours or with a small self-coloured patterned design are a good choice. Cotton is easy to launder, presses well and retains its shape. Three contrasting colours will readily define the abstract forms within the completed design. (The Crazy Log Cabin quilt in the colour photographs was made from fabrics printed by Quilters Treasure - www.quilterstreasure.com. This company has patented an innovative method for creating a marbled design on fabric.)

Thread selection

For economy, select a **regular** weight polyester serging/overlocking thread in a neutral or mid-tone colour such as beige or grey.

For four 19 cm (7½") squares: you need
Four 8 cm (**3"**) squares (for the centre)
Two 4 x 115 cm (**1½ x 45"**) strips* (colour **A**)
Three 4 x 115 cm (**1½ x 45"**) strips* (colour **B**)
Two 5 x 115 cm (**2 x 45"**) strips* (colour **A**)
Two 5 x 115 cm (**2 x 45"**) strips* (colour **B**)
(*All strips are cut across the fabric - selvedge to selvedge. Trim the selvedge from the fabric before cutting the strips.)

Serger Settings: Regular (Select three or four thread overlock option - page 9)

READ CAREFULLY: There is one rule that has to be followed for this method of Crazy Log Cabin: Every strip that is attached MUST cover the underlying fabric from one side to the other.

*_More is better than less for this type of construction technique_*

1. Using colour **A**:
Lay one strip at a slight angle (R/S down) across one of the 8 cm (**3"**) squares (R/S up). Cut the strip just beyond the underlying material. Sew along the raw edge of the strip (blade trims excess fabric outside the edge of the strip).

Turn the strip back. Finger-press the seam (turn seams towards the outer edge).

Place the remainder of the strip (R/S down) across the square at another angle. (Outer edge of strip aligned with underlying fabric.) Cut the strip just beyond the underlying fabric. Sew along the raw edge of the strip (blade trims excess material). Turn the second strip back. Finger-press the seam towards the outer edge.

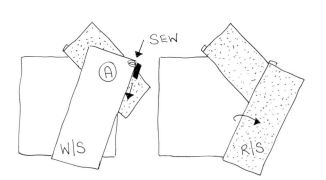

2. Using colour **B**:
Lay one strip at a slightly different angle (R/S down) to the second piece covering all the underlying fabric. Cut the strip. Sew the edge of the strip (blade trims excess fabric).

Turn the strip back. Finger-press the seam (turn seams towards the outer edge).

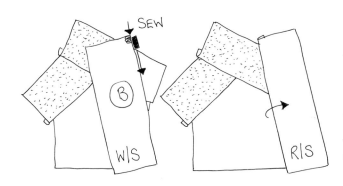

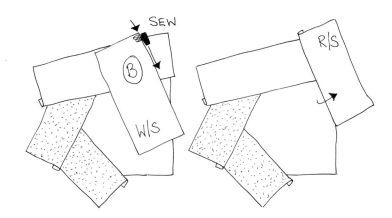

Add a second piece of colour **B** (R/S down). Place at an angle. Cut, sew and turn back, finger-press etc.

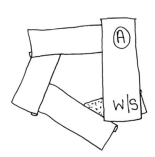

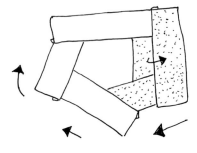

Position one last piece (colour **B** - R/S down). This last strip completes the border. Cut, sew and fold back as before. The centre shape is now surrounded with strips.

3. Press the block well.

That is it!
The border of strips is repeated until the design reaches the required size.
Easy - peasy!

4. Repeat Stages 2 & 3 attaching another complete border of 4 cm (**1½"**) strips: i.e. Two strips colour **A**, three strips colour **B**. (Each time a strip is added it should be the same colour as the strip beneath.) Press well

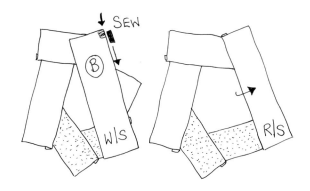

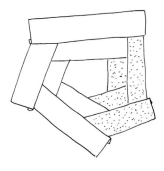

5. Complete the block with another complete border of 5 cm (**2"**) strips: i.e. Two strips colour **A**, three strips colour **B** Press well.

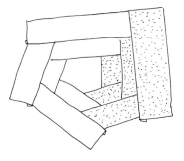

6. Trim the block to make a 19 cm (**7½"**) square. (The square Perspex rulers are very helpful. These come in a variety of sizes and are available from many craft or sewing stores. If you haven't got one, make a 19 cm (**7½"**) cardboard template. Lay the template on the material, draw round, cut on the drawn line.)

Tip: If you can't cut the piece to the suggested size - increase the size by adding a little extra material where needed or cut a smaller square.
:o)

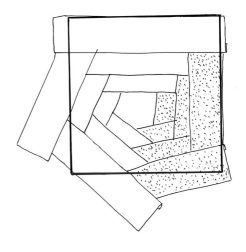

7. Make three more 19 cm (**7½"**) blocks.

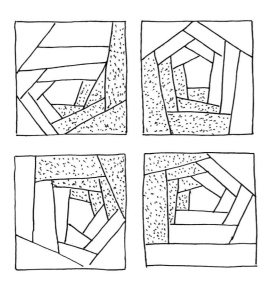

8. Arrange the four blocks to form a large square. There are several different combinations. Choose which one you prefer. Have a play!

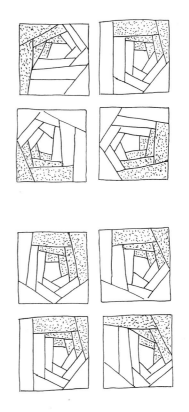

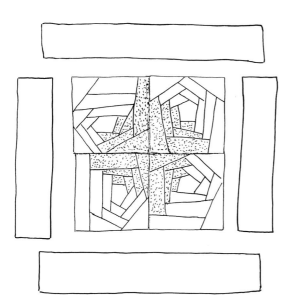

9. Sew the blocks together (page 66). The blade is now used to trim the whiskers off the material and nothing else. No carving great lumps off those neatly cut squares!

Add a border then make the completed panel into a cushion/pillow, a small hanging, cot quilt or a table mat.

Tip: *For a well-stuffed cushion/pillow, buy a pad 2.5 cm **(1")** larger than the completed cover.*

Manmade fibres or feathers for cushion pads - which is better ?

For those with animal or dust allergies manmade fibres are the best, and I would advise buying hypoallergenic fillings. In my opinion, feather cushion pads are more comfortable for resting one's weary head upon. Wash the feather pads occasionally as the feathers get grubby and fusty smelling. Just sling the pad in the washing machine on a gentle (wool) wash then tumble-dry. Tumble drying fluffs the feathers up a treat! I can assure you that nothing disastrous will happen to the feathers. (A lady asked me on one occasion if the feathers shrank and did the colours run? Think of chickens on wet days!)

Play with the pieces

a. Make more squares and turn into a small quilt.

b. Change the colours - use some of the scraps from that overflowing fabric stash and make a multicoloured block.

c. Make the basic block bigger - just add more borders.

d. Change the widths of the attached strips. Make them larger or smaller.

e. Instead of having the seams hidden on the back - have them visible on the front of the design. Thread the serger with black bulk nylon (for good coverage of the raw edges). Lay the strips **R/S** <u>**UP**</u> on to the central shape. Follow the same technique. (See coloured photographs.)

Not that Naff!

Naffness is a particularly British concept. Some innocent and unassuming artefact may be dismissed as 'naff' just because it doesn't suit the viewer's critical judgement. In other words, it lacks refinement, is short on sophistication, slightly vulgar and not quite discerning enough.

Can a person be 'naff'? I don't know but my appearance in the local paper might be considered 'not in the best possible taste'.

Uncover girl

The phone rang. It was a reporter from the local paper. He had seen my name in the list of exhibitors at a national show and realised that I lived near by. Obviously, the editorial staff were short on articles that week. In our conversation, it arose that I had made some unusual clothing - when I mentioned the whip and my black 'strippers' outfit, he instantly arranged to have a photographer round.

I failed to make him appreciate that I was a middle-aged lady but no ..... he felt that a stripping sewer could be good copy. Would I wear my outfit and be ready for the photographer? Well........a lovely tall handsome young man arrived and boy, did I swing into sparkling mode. Flirty Gerty wasn't in it - just as well my man was at home beavering away in his study so I had to behave - sort of!

This young man had me lying on the sofa draped in various poses. Whip in hand, thigh boots and fish net tights to the fore. He smiled and I twinkled. For some reason, I had to make 'big eyebrows'! Then, he wanted a few outdoor shots - in the garden. We don't have a garden so I suggested the street. Next thing I know, I am wrapped round the lamppost, whip in teeth, leg held high making 'big eyebrows' for all I am worth. Two builder chappies drove past in their van, hesitated, whistled, drove to end of road and returned. "Here luv, fancy a bit". Fortunately, the photographer had finished so I fled back to the safety of my own house and climbed back into my usual workday clothes. Next week - who was centre page spread? Yes, it was I! I might never make page three in the national newspapers due to lack of chest, beauty and age, but I have been pages 21 and 22 in our local rag.

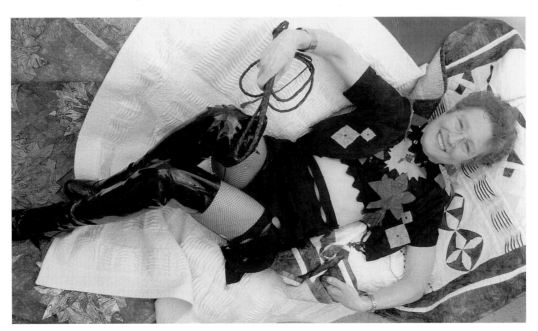

Tissue box cover

Beautify the boudoir, pretty up the powder room: decorate the dressing table or vanity unit with this delectable tissue box cover. A most excellent gift for Mother's Day. *(The tissue box cover is definitely one up on the crocheted crinoline lady on the loo roll - that really is naff!)*

Material choice

Two contrasting coloured materials can be combined if desired. <u>The majority of the box exterior is constructed from one colour</u>; the other colour is displayed in the central square windows on each side.

Select a firmly woven medium weight material that is **reversible** or one that has a pleasing wrong side (both R/S and W/S will show) for the **main** part of the box. Plain glazed cotton (chintz), gabardine, linen, silk or one of the hand dyed batiks would be ideal. Why not use some leftover curtain/drape material and make a box to match the room decor?

Thread selection

For an attractive exterior finish to the box choose threads that contrast with the main material. Floss, metallic or variegated thread is ideal - gird up your loins (no sniggering, I wrote 'lions' in the first proof!) and re-thread the machine (page 9 for easy method).

You need

*(All metreage/yardage cut from 112/115 cm (**44/45"**) width fabric.*
35 cm (**12"**) fabric - main colour
17 cm (**6"**) fabric - supplementary colour
Contrasting coloured and matching threads to fabric
Cube box of tissues/Kleenex

Tissue Box with tissues!
13 cm (5")
Firm woven batik
R/S and W/S shown

Jennie Rayment

1. Cut from main colour: Ten 15 cm (5¾") squares. Cut all ten squares diagonally in half forming triangles.

2. Cut from secondary colour: Four 15 cm (5¾") squares.

3. Using the rolled hem setting on the serger (see below), sew the bias (stretchy) side of all the triangles. Should the chosen material have one side subtly different to the other, decide on which side is the W/S and keep the W/S uppermost while sewing. Press the stitched edge of the triangles gently on completion of the sewing.

Serger Settings: Rolled Hem

Needle: Remove left needle
Blade: Engaged - set at normal
Tensions: Tighten lower looper - 7/9
Stitch Length: Reduce to smaller stitch length
Stitch width: Narrow. Retract stitch finger (page 12)

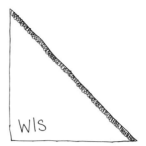

4. Take **four** of the triangles and one 15 cm (5¾") square. Lay the 15 cm (5¾") square on a flat surface R/S up. Follow the diagrams below.

a. Position one triangle R/S up with the right-angled corner of the triangle on the left-hand side of the square, aligning all raw edges. Insert a pin in the right-hand corner of the triangle. (Pin goes through the triangle not through the square.)

b. Place a second triangle on top of the first; rotate this one through 90° (a quarter turn), turning in a **clockwise** direction keeping the folded edge towards the centre. The pin is still visible and part of the 15 cm (5¾") square shows.

c. Place a third triangle on top of the second and rotate in the same manner (through 90°). Pin is still visible but the square is completely covered.

d. Finally, the fourth triangle is placed on top of the third one and rotated through 90°. **The pin is concealed**. Tuck the left-hand corner of this triangle under the first one to **reveal the pin**! The stitched edges of the triangles form a diagonal cross. Remove the pin.

e. Ensure that all the raw edges of the triangles and the base square are aligned. A small gap at the centre does not matter. Pin all the layers carefully with eight pins, two either side of each diagonal fold. Keep pins away from raw edges. The stitched edges of the triangles should lie side by side and not overlap each other.

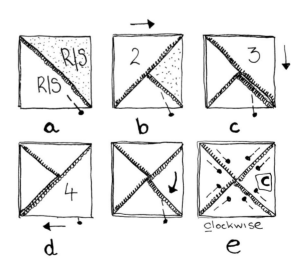

5. Using four more triangles, make another block - take care to rotate **clockwise**.

*Tip: Avoid confusion - label these completed blocks **C** (for **Clockwise**).*

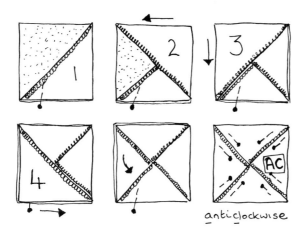

anticlockwise

6. Make a third block using four more triangles **BUT** .... Rotate these triangles round **ANTI -(COUNTER) CLOCKWISE** - follow the diagram.

Place the right-angled corner of the triangle on the right of the background square; **put the pin in the** left-hand corner. Remember that these pieces are rotated round **anti-(counter) clockwise - rotate the pieces towards the pin**.)

7. As in Stage 2, pin the layers on the corners. Label this block **AC** (**A**nti-**C**lockwise).

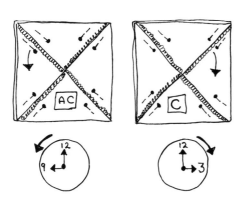

8. Repeat Stage 7 to make one more anti-clockwise rotated block.

9. Check the mirror imaging - lay one **anti-(counter) clockwise** (**AC**) and one **clockwise** (**C**) block side by side. **The stitched edges roll back in opposite directions**.

Four triangles remain. Panic not! These are for the top of the box.

10. Alter the serger settings - see below. Re-thread with a colour that matches the main fabric.

Serger Settings: Narrow seam

Needle: Right-hand needle only - remove left-hand one
Blade: Engaged - set at normal
Tensions: Normal
Stitch Length: Maximum
Stitch width: Medium - set stitch finger to midpoint

Tip: Using only one needle and one thread creates a less dense stitch. If both needles are threaded, the stitching is much heavier. Heavy (dense) stitching makes bulky seams.

Using the longest stitch length available, baste the raw edges of the four blocks. Keep basting as close to the raw edge as possible. Remove pins as you sew.

11. Arrange the four blocks as a strip <u>alternating <u>C</u>lockwise and <u>A</u>nti- (counter)</u>
<u>C</u>lockwise units.

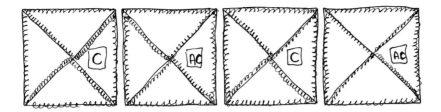

12. **<u>Replace and re-thread serger left-hand needle</u>.**
<u>Reduce the stitch length to the normal setting</u>. Sew
the blocks together using 1 cm ($^3/_8$") S/A. Align the
stitched edges of the triangles carefully. Trim the
fabric whiskers with the blade. On one side of the
strip, leave 1 cm ($^3/_8$") unsewn at the end of each
seam.

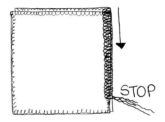

*Tip: Sew down one seam, stop 1 cm (3/8") approximately from the end of the seam. Raise
needles, lift presser foot and pull work out. Chain off (continue to stitch). Cut threads.
Repeat with the next seam etc.*

Manipulating the triangles
*This section can be completed now (by hand or sewing machine), or left until the tissue
box cover is finished then hand sewn in place. It is easier to roll the edges of all the
triangles and stitch in place at this stage.*

1. Roll back the stitched edge of each triangle in an arc as far as possible. The underlying
square will be revealed in the gap between the rolled edges. Roll each edge by the same
amount to form a square window. Pin in place and press.

2. On the seams where
the rolled edges touch,
secure with a few
stitches. Sew through all
the layers either by hand
or on the sewing
machine.

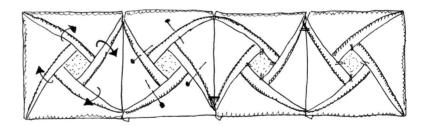

*Tip: Three options for
machine sewers:*

      *a. Set a short stitch length (0.5 - 1.0) on the sewing machine. Sew forwards and
      backwards across the rolled edge twice. Trim thread ends.*

*Or   b. Use the fix setting on the machine - **reduce the stitch length to 0** before you press
      fix. Press fix twice for maximum effectiveness.*

*Or   c. Attach the free embroidery/darning/hopper foot, lower or cover feed dogs. Sew on
      the spot fractionally moving the fabric. Leave the threads connected and jump to
      next place, repeat etc. On completion, trim threads flush on the R/S and leave a
      small tail on W/S.*

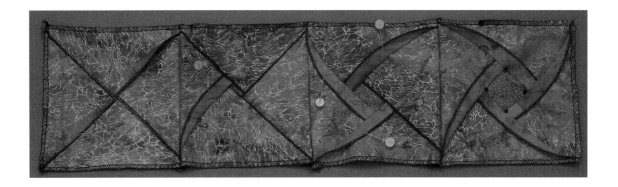

If you prefer to sew by hand - why not add a bead or two at the same time?

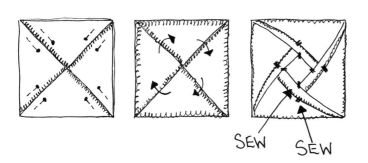

SEW SEW

Making the tissue box top
1. Take the last four 15 cm (5¾") triangles. Construct one more block for the top following Stage 4 page 33 but omit the square.

2. Baste round the raw edge as described in Stage 10 (increase the stitch length).

3. Roll back the stitched edge of all four triangles to form a square. Sew the stitched edge in place where indicated in the diagram.

Construct the box
1. Sew ends of the strip together to make a tube. Leave 1 cm (³/₈") unsewn at start of seam. Try not to catch the rolled edges of the triangles in the seam - pin flat if necessary. Leave the tube W/S out.

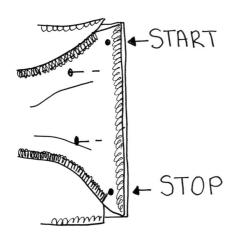

START

STOP

2. Pin the tissue box top in place, matching the sides of the top with the sides of the box. Pin R/Ss together.

3. Start and stop the stitching 1 cm (³/₈") from either end of each seam. (This is a bit of a jiggle on the serger/overlocker, but you could complete this step on the sewing machine or even - perish the thought - by hand!) Turn R/S out.

Tip: Should a small gap be visible on the corner junctions - a spot of hand stitching will repair the damage!

4. Serge round the raw edge of the base of the box. Keep the stitch width at maximum but reduce the stitch length to minimum. Stitch carefully over the seams. Trim any uneven edges with the blade as you sew round.

Tip: For a decorative finish and good coverage of the raw edge, include ribbon in the stitching.
Select a narrow ribbon (6 mm/¼″ width) in the same colour as the thread. Pin the ribbon flush with the edge. Serge/overlock over the ribbon. The raw ends of the ribbon will get covered in the stitching.

5. Fit the cover over the box of tissues/Kleenex and pull the tissues through the hole in box top. Remember to open the tissue box first. *:o)*

Ideas for development

a. This design can be made from any size of triangles. For bigger blocks - cut larger squares! Why not combine different materials in a variety of colours? Thickly woven fabrics can be used for bigger blocks, and fine silks, gauzes and voiles for smaller blocks.

b. Triangles were used for the tissue box to reduce the seam bulk but this design can also be made from squares folded diagonally to form triangles. Although the end product is bulkier, any fabric can be incorporated - it does not have to be reversible. Why not cut some squares and make a cushion front? Ideal for a quick gift.

Quickie cushion with squares

Cut five 25 cm (**10″**) squares. Fold four squares diagonally to form triangles. Overlock the diagonal edge with narrow seam (insert left hand needle only) or rolled hem setting. Make one block following Stages 3-4 page 33. Baste the raw edges before adding a border.

To complete the cushion: Mount the panel on to wadding/batting. Pin the layers together. Set the stitch length to maximum and sew round the outside edge so basting[P1] the layers together. Attach a backing. Remember to pin backing and cushion panel R/S's together.

Sew the backing on to the cushion front, sewing round the corners in a gentle arc. Leave a gap along one edge. Turn the cushion cover through the gap. Stuff in the cushion pad. Stitch the gap together by hand. Violà! An instant present.

Why not add more colours for a really impressive cushion?
Take two different coloured fabrics and cut two 25 cm (**10″**) squares from both materials. Divide all four squares into triangles.

Sew two different coloured triangles together (**R/Ss out)** to make a square. Fold in half and sew the diagonal edge with narrow seam (right-hand needle only or use rolled hem setting (page 33). Press the seam.

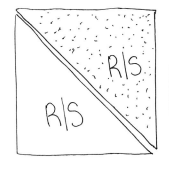 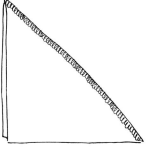

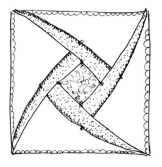

Cut one more 25 cm (**10"**) square from another fabric. Follow Stage 4 page 33. Arranging each with the same colour uppermost. Baste the raw edge. Add a border.

Roll back the stitched edges to reveal the other colour. Stitch the rolled edges in place.

Quickie cushion with an extra twiddle

1. Cut four 25 cm (**10"**) squares from a reversible material (both R/S and W/S will show on the cushion front).

2. Follow Stages 1 - 4 pages 58 - Sewing Caddy Front.

3. Cut one more 25 cm (**10"**) square.

4. Make up one block as described in Stage 4 page 33.

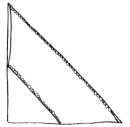 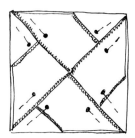 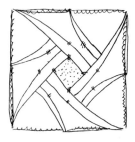

5. Roll back the four folds in the centre AND the smaller fold on each corner.

Secure the folds with a small hand stitch, or try tips suggested on page 35.

6. Add a border, backing, and push a pad in. It's a quickie cushion with an extra twiddle.

Cushion Front
*40 cm (**16"**)*
Jennie Rayment

Quags and Quillows

What is a Quag? Well it is a quillow with handles. No wiser? Read through the next few pages to find out.

Ooh la la!!

Not that long ago, I was invited to a quilt exhibition in Lyons. What a delight - fly to France and demonstrate for three days. I was really chuffed to be asked.

Flew to Lyons, landed and then remembered that I don't speak French - he does. Whenever I have been to France, it has been with the man. He speaks the lingo. I just smile and say "Merci, s'il vous plaît, por favor and taeverso" or any other odd expression I can conjure up at that moment. Did I pack a dictionary? No. Never mind, I am a big girl now, I can cope.

Hailed a cab and showed the guy the address of the show. He bundled me into the back of the cab and we drove at a fast and furious speed out of the city. Was I being abducted? White slave traffic? Oh dear! Then I remembered that I was a middle-aged woman of no interest whatsoever to any would be kidnapper or slave trafficker.

He drove towards some enormous old brick warehouses in a semi-industrial area. I could see lots of white vans parked nearby. These must be the vans delivering all the goods to the show. Oh we were nearly there, I bounced up and down in my seat in excitement, pointed and exclaimed, "Monsieur, voilà (or did I say viola) le quilt show. Il est ici!" (French is my strong subject!) The cabby looked horrified and said very slowly, "Madame, les dames de nuit!"

Ladies of the night! I looked more closely. All the vehicles were immaculately presented. Pretty lace curtains hung at the windows and some of the vans had small vases of flowers on the dashboard. They all looked charming. Each little van was parked a parking space apart thereby providing easy movement of the 'guests', extra privacy for any noisy and over-enthusiastic visitors and sufficient space for the vans to sway in moments of passion. How very sensible of the French authorities to house their 'loose knickered' ladies or those of easy virtue in a small commune outside the city boundary.

Unfortunately, some of the visitors to the quilt show were most unhappy and made extremely vociferous objections about the location. The exhibition has now been moved to another venue.

C'est la vie!

Quags and quillows

Quillows are quilts that fold up into a cushion or pillow. It is 'two for the price of one' - both a soft supportive cushion when folded and a comfy cuddly covering when opened out. Why not sling one on the sofa for cold winter evenings to keep your toes cosy, give one to an elderly relative to snuggle under or throw one in the car for the children to snooze beneath?

The quillow or as some call it - a secret pillow has been around for a long time, I forget who first thought of it but the quag is a 'Jennie' idea. I get these daft notions occasionally! The basic quillow design consists of a quilt with a panel stitched on the back (the measurement of the sides of the panel is one third of the measurement of the sides of the quilt). The panel is sewn onto the quilt on three sides. By a simple method of folding, the quilt can be inserted into the open side of the panel making a soft cushion or pillow. It is a really nifty notion.

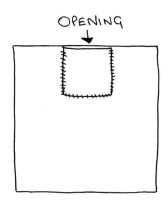

A quag is the same basic concept but has handles; it becomes a bag not a pillow! It is a brilliant accessory for travellers. There is room in the bag panel of the quag for your book, sandwiches, bottle of whatever and other vital travel accoutrements. It is absolutely ideal for the aircraft. Planes are often extremely chilly and the regulation airline blankets are remarkably thin. If you get cold, place the contents of the quag in the seat pocket, turn the quag inside out and tuck the enclosed quilt over your knees. Bliss!

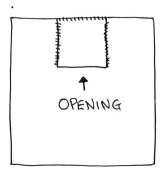

Take a quag on a picnic or to the beach - carry the food in the bag then unfold the quag to produce a picnic cloth or beach mat. Why not celebrate the birth of a baby by giving a quag to the new parents? Not only will the bag hold lots of baby paraphernalia but the enclosed quilt also makes an excellent mat for the babe to lie on.

The ratio of the sides of the panel to the quilt when making a quag does not have to be 1:3. These proportions are necessary when making a quillow to ensure that the quilt forms a nice plump pillow when folded into the cover. For quags, making the quilt smaller and the attached panel larger than one third is preferable - more space for toting all the stuff!

Only two layers are used to make the quag: fabric for the top and fleece for the backing. *(Ardent quilters may wish to substitute the fleece for a layer of wadding/batting and a backing fabric. The same construction method applies.)*

Fabric choice
Select a hard wearing washable fabric and a good quality fleece. Wash both the fabric and the fleece beforehand to prevent the dye colours running and any further shrinkage of the materials.

To make a quillow: Follow the same instructions but increase the quilt size to 150 cm (60") and omit the handles.

For a 120 cm (48") square quag: you need
Quilt: One 120 cm **(48")** square - fabric
       One 120 cm **(48")** square - fleece
Panel: One 50 cm **(20")** square - fabric
       One 50 cm **(20")** square - fleece
Handles: Two 50 x 10 cm **(20 x 4")** strips
Thread to match fabrics

Serger Settings: Regular
(Select three/four thread overlock option - page 10)

1. <u>Make the handles</u>: Fold one of the 50 x 10 cm **(20 x 4")** strips in half widthways. Serge both long sides. Repeat with the other strip. (For added strength and extra padding, enclose a layer of wadding.)

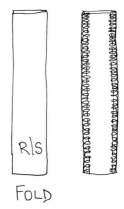

2. <u>Make the quilt</u>: Lay the fleece (W/S up) on the floor or a large table. Secure the sides of the fleece by pushing pins through the fleece into the carpet or by taping the edges down with masking tape or a similar product.

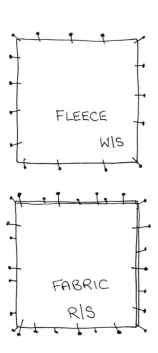

3. Place the fabric square (R/S up) on top of the fleece. Align all the raw edges. Use safety pins to anchor the layers together. Place the pins at 15 cm **(6")** intervals approximately. Be generous with the pins on the outside edges.

Tip: Substitute a Tak gun for safety pins: (This is an ingenious gadget that pushes small plastic tags through layers of material.) For maximum anchorage of the layers weave the needle in through both layers and back out again on top before firing the tag. Tak guns are available in many craft or quilt stores (photograph page 13).

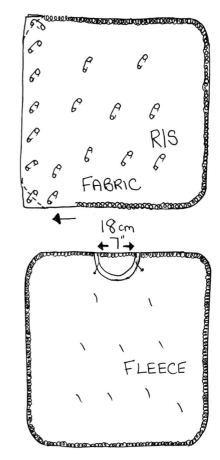

4. Draw a gentle curve on the corners of the quilt. Sew round the raw edge, trimming the corners to the drawn line with the blade. Don't forget to remove the pins on the edge as you sew - do not stitch over pins.

5. Pin one of the handle sections to the <u>fleece</u> side (back) of the quilt. Align the raw ends of the handle with the edge of the quilt and set the ends of the handle approximately 18 cm **(7")** apart. Reduce the stitch length to minimum. Stitch slowly over the handle ends.

6. <u>Make the panel</u>: Repeat Stages 2 and 3 with the two remaining 50 cm (**20"**) fabric and fleece squares.

7. Pin the handle on the <u>fabric</u> side (R/S) of the panel setting the ends approximately 18 cm (**7"**) apart.

P.S. Good idea to have the handle on the panel and quilt set apart the same distance. :o)

8. Sew round the panel. Reduce the stitch length when sewing over the handles. Leave the corners square. Try the Pam Neave corner trick (page 14).

9. Anchor both layers of the quilt and the panel with a few small hand stitches. Stitch the layers together approximately every 15 cm (**6"**). Use a complimentary or a contrasting thread. Alternatively, hold the layers in place with a quilting tie.

Quilting Tie: *A really complicated technique!* Thread a needle with any thread you choose. Pass the needle through all the layers; bring the needle back up making a small stitch. Pull the thread through leaving a 10 cm (**4"**) tail. Repeat the stitching using same holes. Cut thread approximately 10 cm (**4"**) from the stitches. Tie the ends firmly together using a reef/square knot..

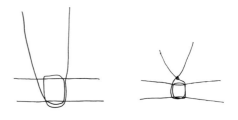

Alternatively, secure the two layers with buttons, beads and even small tassels. The choice of embellishment depends on what you intend to do with the quag. (No rude ripostes please)

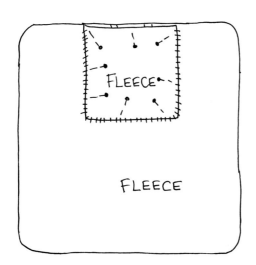

Complete the quag
1. Place the <u>fabric side of the panel on the fleece side of the quilt.</u> Align both handles. Pin the panel to the quilt carefully. (The handles are sandwiched between the panel and the quilt.)

2.The panel is sewn on to the quilt on three sides (see the diagram). **SADLY**, this next stage ought to be done by hand (making a face like a dog chewing a wasp at this suggestion is unnecessary, some people like doing things by hand!) **BUT**..... it is possible to use a cover stitch serger (page 19) or a sewing machine....Read on..........

By hand: Sew round the panel. Use a strong thread and stitch firmly through all the layers. Keep the stitching to the edge of the panel. The choice of stitch is irrelevant - just anchor the layers neatly and securely.

By sewing machine: Pin both layers together thoroughly. The best presser foot would be a 'walking foot' (see instruction book), or engage the even-feed foot (Pfaff owners only). If you don't possess either type of foot use the regular presser foot, sew slowly and check that both layers remain stable and neither one creeps. Sometimes slackening off the presser foot control is helpful (not all machines have this option.) Sew round the sides of the panel with a medium length but narrow zigzag or a medium length straight stitch (no wobbling).

Be aware: The stitching on the sewing machine and a cover stitch serger shows on the fabric side of the quilt - does it matter? Heavily patterned materials will absorb the pattern, plain ones will reveal it.

Tip: *Threading the bobbin or both loopers with invisible/nylon thread will disguise the stitching on the underside.*

Fold the quag

The quag can now be folded into the panel section on the back of the quilt. This is the magic part. Try it - it does work - have faith, read the words and look at the diagrams!

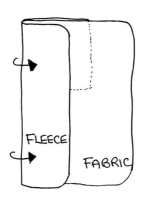
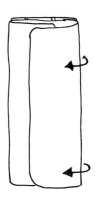

1. Open out the quilt. Lay it on a flat surface <u>with the fleece side underneath; quilt on the top (fabric side of quilt uppermost)</u>.

2. Fold both sides over on the panel seam. The two sides will overlap.

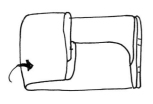

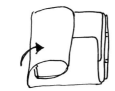

3. Fold the quilt end to touch the panel. Fold the quilt once more creating a neat 'package' on top of the panel.

4. Flip the entire package over. The panel (fleece side) is now on top. Thrust your hands into the bag section (between the panel and the quilt); grab the corners of the folded quilt and pull them through the opening turning the bag inside out. The quilt remains inside the bag panel. At first, it's a bit of a wrestle but with practice becomes much easier.

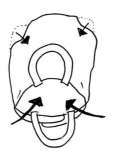

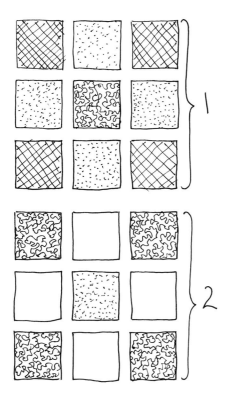

Ideas for development

a. Patchwork quags:

Join a selection of strips, squares, other geometric shapes and/or your favourite block design etc. to make one large piece of material. There is no reason why a Sudoku (page 63) could not be turned into the quilt section of a quag.

Alternatively make a simple nine-patch design:

1. Arrange nine squares (cut from three or four different colours) in two basic pattern formats as shown in the diagram. (Follow Stage 4 on page 66 for instructions on sewing the squares together.)

2. Make five blocks from one colour arrangement and four blocks of the other. Form a large square with the nine completed blocks. Lay the blocks out in a pleasing formation. Sew all the blocks together (follow Stage 6 page 66 onwards).

3. Make the bag panel in a similar design.

A further option: Why not construct a quag from a UFO (unfinished object)? Most sewers have several languishing in the cupboard or gathering dust in a corner. Does the panel have to match the quilt? Surely another UFO or any other bit of material could be suitable.

b. Alter the dimensions of the panel and/or the quilt:
The minimum size of the quag bag panel is one-third of the measurements of the quilt sides (the same proportions as the quillow). Making the bag panel larger than this minimum measurement creates more room for all the junk you have to tote around. More is always better than less most of the time, or so I tell 'him indoors'!

c. Adjust the handle size:
The handle strips can be any lengths you choose. To make a strong (or to shorten) handle: fold the handle in a pleat at the junction of the handle and the quilt/bag panel. Stitch a button to both sides through all the layers.

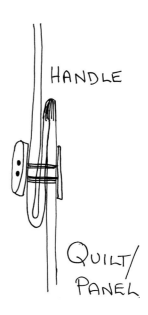

HANDLE

QUILT/ PANEL

Serge into Caddies

The importance of milk

I have to confess to being a teatotaller. No, not a teetotaller, but I am totally addicted to those dried leaves containing tannin. Life for me is not a bowl of cherries but a cup of tea. Providing I have some tea bags, a kettle, a mug and the all-important milk then I can cope with most things. These days I have kettles (hot jugs) in a variety of voltages for different parts of the world and would never dream of setting forth without the relevant kettle for that country's power supply. Tea bags travel in my luggage and if I run out (shock, horror!) most places have some form of regular tea in the local supermarket. Plain old Indian tea, even the floor sweepings from the tea factory are fine as I like my brew weak. You can keep all the fancy flavoured varieties like Earl Grey although I will drink peppermint tea in desperation. In my opinion, chamomile is much better left in the garden, in fact if I wanted to drink grass cuttings I would mow the lawn.

Tea has to have fresh milk and, dare I confess, sugar. Sugar is readily available; most fast food places have baskets of little packets just waiting to be collected. Getting hold of fresh milk is the problem. I have walked miles in many foreign parts of the world to find a supply. Macdonalds sell it by the carton, as do most garages (gas stations in US), which is a big advantage. I recall hoofing three miles down the edge of a particularly busy American freeway then discovering the garage was on the other side. Undaunted, I ran rapidly across the road to reach the central reservation, vaulted the barrier then dashed madly to safety. Bought my milk and then had to repeat the somewhat perilous journey. Was it worth it? Yes!

Wandering across the lobby of a very posh New Hampshire hotel to find my room, a hand tapped me on the shoulder and a voice said quietly, "Mam! You are leaking!" I turned and saw across the lobby and as far as the eye could see was a small trail of milk. The precious carton of milk must have turned turtle in my baggage. What a waste!

A similar occurrence, whilst on a car rally in the Austrian Alps…. We were waiting in the car for the next section to start when a chap came up to the car and said "Excuse me, but there appears to be something dripping from your back suspension". "Good Lord!" exclaimed the man, leaping out of the E-type, immediately visualising some awful disaster like brake fluid or fuel seeping from a pipe. He need not have worried, my bottle of milk had fallen over in the boot (trunk for all those over the water) and the liquid was trickling out of a corner, down through a crack and was emerging by the back wheel. You can imagine his relief when he discovered it was milk and not anything untoward, although he was not exactly delighted about the spillage!

DRAWN BY NICK

Serge into caddies

In case you are wondering what a caddy is, here is a brief explanation.

According to the dictionary, it is a container, rack or other device for holding, storing or organising items. Possibly the best known caddy is the tea caddy. The word probably originated in the mid 1800's and was a derivation of 'catty'. A catty was a Chinese and Southeast Asian measure, weighing about 680 grams (1½ pounds). Tea leaves were weighed in catties, packed in boxes ready for sale. The transition from 'catty' to 'caddy' is simple to envisage and so the tea caddy came into existence.

Rest assured that these caddies do not have to contain tea leaves or even tea bags but can be filled with useful bits and bobs or left empty as a decorative dust collector!

If you prefer call all the designs in this chapter 'boxes' not caddies, feel free. The word box came from the French - 'boîte' and they got it from Latin - 'buxis'. It is amazing how words move through different countries and change over the centuries.

All of the caddies shown on the next few pages can be made in any size, are simple to construct, quick to make, and as a bonus are reversible - you can select which side is to be on the outside. They make ideal gifts for friends and relatives, particularly those who live overseas. A completed caddy weighs very little and can be packed flat so it is inexpensive to mail and simple to wrap.

Fabric choice
Select a light/medium-weight fabric that is washable. Press the fabric carefully before cutting to size. Why not make a caddy in scraps of leftover furnishing or curtaining fabric from the guest-room? Fill it with toiletries or other welcoming niceties ready for your next set of visitors. Accessorise the dinner table with a bread roll caddy (line with a cloth or paper napkin to protect the material)! In fact you can put a caddy in most places from the sewing room to the boudoir, or anywhere else you fancy.

Thread Selection
For good coverage of the raw edges, thread the loopers with bulk (woolly) nylon or another thick decorative thread. Regular weight polyester would be suitable for the needles.

Play with a selection of thread colours and types to discover which combination looks attractive on the chosen fabric. Check the stitching on a scrap of interfacing and fabric.

For all the designs featured in this chapter use the following serger settings

Serger Settings

Needles: Thread both or remove right-hand needle (page 10)
Blade: Disengage - or set at furthest distance from needle
Tensions: Regular
Stitch Length: Reduce to smaller stitch length
Stitch width: Widest. Set stitch finger at maximum (page 12)

Square caddy

Finished size of base: 20 cm **(8")** square. Finished depth: 5 cm **(2")**

You need
Two 20 cm **(8")** squares regular or heavy weight fusible interfacing (see page 16/17)
Two 31 cm **(12½")** squares fabric.
Two metres **(2 yards)** thin ribbon
Adhesive or masking tape

1. Cut **one** of the *fusible interfacing squares into four 20 x 5 cm **(8 x 2")** strips.

  ****P.S. Instead of always saying 'fusible interfacing' in this chapter, sometimes I have
shortened it to read 'interfacing' - it is still the same stuff. (Saves typing the word fusible
so much!)***

Completed caddy
Jennie Rayment

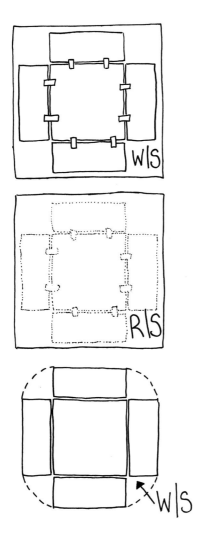

2. Lay one 31 cm (**12½"**) fabric square **W/S** up on a flat surface. Place the 20 cm (**8"**) square of fusible interfacing in the centre. Place one strip on each side of the square leaving a small gap between the pieces.

Stick the fusible interfacing sections together with small pieces of masking or adhesive tape.

3. Turn the fabric and the taped pieces over onto the ironing board (R/S of fabric on top - fusible interfacing beneath). Take care - don't disturb the tape.

Tip: Slide a thin board or ruler under the fabric then flip over - like tossing a pancake!

Press the fabric to the fusible interfacing sections (ensure that the fabric is still covering the interfacing sections). Press slowly with a hot dry iron. Try not to singe the material.

4. Remove the tape. Trim the excess material to the outside edges of the fusible interfacing strips. Trim all four corners in a gentle arc

Tip: Use any circular object as a template i.e. the base of your coffee/tea mug or small plate.

5. Press the second 31 cm (**12½"**) square on the other side of the fusible interfacing. Trim the excess material (Stage 4). Pin both layers on the rounded corners. Keep the pins away from the fabric edge.

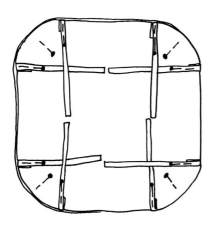

6. Cut the ribbon into eight equal lengths. Take one piece and fold one end over by approximately 1.5 cm (**½"**). Pin this end to the raw edge of the caddy on the end of the interfacing strip. Repeat with the other seven lengths - one length at each end.

7. Remember to test the serger stitching on a small scrap of fusible interfacing and fabric. (Ensure the blade is disengaged or set at the farthest distance from the stitching.)

8. Start the overlock stitching immediately beside one of the pinned pieces of ribbon. Sew carefully along the raw edge. Keep the folded edge of the ribbon away from the blade (the folded end of the ribbon is covered by the stitching). Remove the pins as you sew. Be very careful as you approach the start of the stitching, do not let the blade cut through the original sewing.

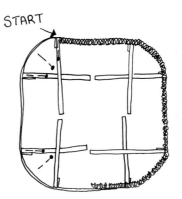

Sew slowly round the arced corners.

Tip: Sew a small section, drop the needle/s into the fabric, turn the work slightly, sew another short section and repeat. Sewing round any arc in small sections is much easier than whizzing round the corner, flying off the edge and generally getting in a pickle. Sometimes slow is better than fast. Not often!

9. On completion of the stitching, raise presser foot; pull the work away from under the presser foot. Chain off. Secure the thread ends (page 13).

10. Trim any excess ribbon away from the stitching line.

11. Decide which side of the caddy is the outer side. Fold the sides together and tie the ribbons with a small reef knot (right ribbon over left, left ribbon over right). Tie the remaining length in a bow.

Trim all the ribbon ends in a neat V shape or at an angle to prevent the raw ends fraying.

12. Fold the corners of the caddy back to reveal the inner colour.

Fill the caddy with odd and bobs. It is a most excellent repository for all those little bottles of shampoo, conditioner and lotion that one acquires when travelling.

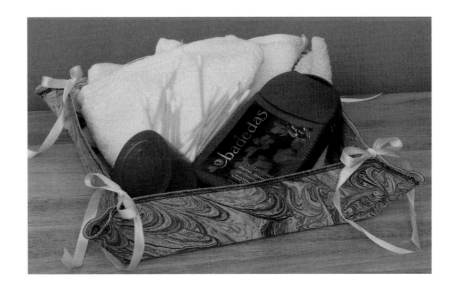

Try a subtly different design

1. Omit the ribbon. Start the stitching in the same place and sew round raw edge as described in Stage 8.

2. Fold the sides of the caddy together; sew across the corners with a few firm stitches. Add a bead at the same time.

3. Open the corners and flatten into a cone shape. Sew the sides of the flattened corner to the sides of the caddy (top drawing).

Alternatively, open the corners; pull the midpoint downwards. Secure the midpoint and the sides with a few stitches. Roll open the two folds and sew in place.

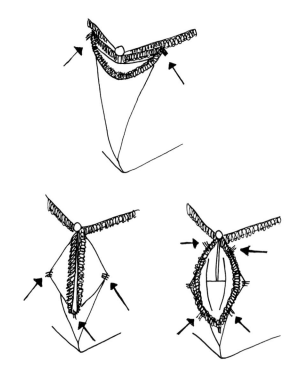

Three different ways of completing the caddy corners

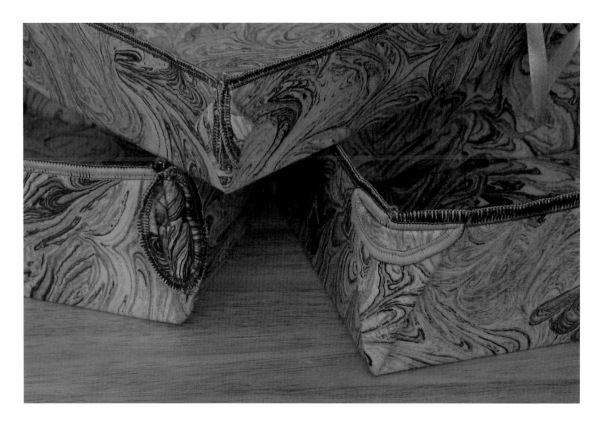

Caddy with a lid on top

You need:
Six 10 cm (**4"**) squares regular or heavy weight
fusible interfacing (see page16/17)
Two 31 cm (**12½"**) squares fabric.
Two 12 cm (**5"**) squares fabric
Adhesive or masking tape

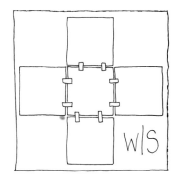

1. Arrange the 10 cm (**4"**) squares of fusible
interfacing on one of the 31 cm (**12½"**) squares
as shown in the diagram. Use small lengths of
masking or adhesive tape to stick the interfacing
sections together.

2. Follow instructions given in Stages 3 - 5 on
page 48.

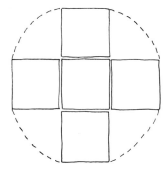

3. <u>Make the lid</u>: Press one 12 cm (**5"**) fabric to
one side of the remaining fusible interfacing
square. Trim the fabric level with the interfacing.
Press another piece of material on the other side.
Trim the edges level.

4. Serge the raw edges. Chain off each side or try the Pam Neave corner trick (page 14).
Tidy the thread ends (page 13).

Tip: *Prevent the lid falling in the box, by adding a few beads to the corners of the lid.*

A further thought ...... Reinforce the lid by adding a smaller piece of fusible interfacing to
the underside or an additional piece to the top. Attach to the lid with a few hand stitches
(perish the thought!) or a fabric glue. It is possible to sew the sections in place on the
sewing machine if you have no objection to the stitching showing on one side or the other.

Finally embellish
the top and/or the
sides with a few
3D flowers (page
71). Attach by
hand or for a faster
option - use glue!

Why not attach the caddy lid?

The lid can be stitched to the caddy by hand or on the serger using a flatlock seam. Take a deep breath - the settings will have to be altered.

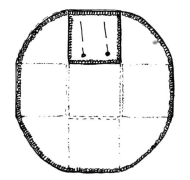

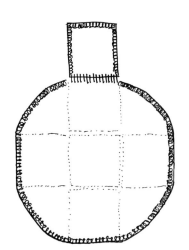

Serger Settings: Flatlock

Needles: Remove right-hand needle
Blade: Disengage
Tensions: Loosen left-hand needle tension - turn to lowest number
Tighten lower looper - turn to highest number
Stitch Length: Reduce to smaller stitch length
Stitch width: Widest. Set stitch finger at maximum (page 12)

Test the stitching on two layers of fusible interfacing - adjust the tensions if needed. Run the edge of the presser foot along the edge of the materials. Changing the needle for a heavy weight fabric one (90/100) is advisable.

1. Pin the lid to the flat caddy base - W/S of lid to W/S of caddy. Be careful to align the lid with the one of the interfacing sections.

2. Flatlock the seam. Tidy the threads ends (see page 13).

3. Hold the lid and pull firmly away from the caddy. The stitching should flatten out - fingers crossed! Should the stitching fail to flatten completely, unpick the seam and attach the lid by hand. A little job to do before falling asleep in front of the television.

Experiment with triangular and hexagonal caddies

Templates for triangles and hexagons can be found on page 103.

1. Cut out the base of the caddy in fusible interfacing. Measure the length of one side of the base. Cut strips of fusible interfacing this length and the desired depth of the caddy.

2. Tape the sections together - remember the gap.

3. Follow the instructions given on pages 48 - 49. Start the stitching on the end of one of the sections of fusible interfacing unless attaching ribbons.

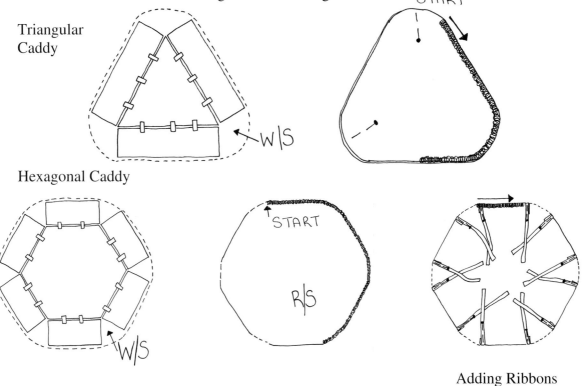

Triangular Caddy

Hexagonal Caddy

Adding Ribbons

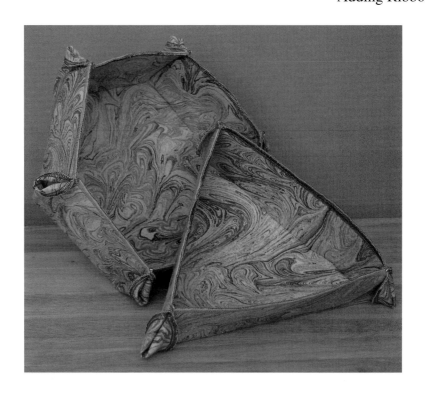

Triangular and Hexagonal Caddies

Try other shapes

Caddies can be made in any geometrical shape. Rectangles are simple: cut the base then cut the strips for the sides. Diamonds, pentagons and other geometric forms usually require a protractor and ruler for the construction of a basic template, but octagons can be created easily.

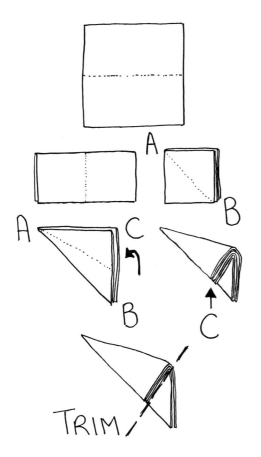

Octagonal template

1. Decide on approximate size of the base of the completed caddy. Cut a square of paper this measurement.

2. Fold the square in half and in half again. Press the creases firmly.

3. Fold diagonally from **A** to **B**. *Beware! A wrong move will result in four pieces of paper not an octagon!* Watch the folds carefully - all folds lie together.

4. Fold diagonally one last time - check all the folds lie together. Trim off the corner.

5. Open out. If you folded the paper properly the shape should be octagonal - if not start again!

<u>To make an octagonal caddy</u>: Use the paper base as a template. Cut the base in fusible interfacing plus eight strips the desired depth and the exact length of the sides of the octagonal base. Follow the same construction technique as the other caddies in this chapter, i.e. tape the fusible interfacing pieces together, press fabric to both sides and trim excess fabric. Serge/overlock the raw edge, with or without ribbon etc. etc. etc. (See coloured photographs.)

Now for something completely different...... Book covers

The same trick of taping sections of fusible interfacing (page 16/17) works remarkably well when it comes to covering a book.

Just think of the benefit - a covered book conceals the content - no-one can see what you are reading. Behind a customised dust jacket, you can happily peruse any book you fancy - the mind boggles!! It might be 'Tucked up in Bed' or 'Serging for Softies'. Qui sait? (French for 'who knows'.)

1. Draw round the book cover on some paper. Add 1 cm ($^3/_8$") to both ends and one side of the drawing. Cut two pieces of fusible interfacing this size.

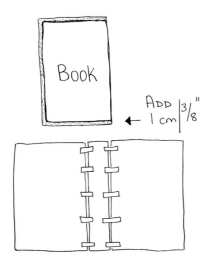

Measure the width of the spine. Cut one piece of fusible interfacing this width and the same length as the cover sections. Tape the pieces together leaving a small gap between the three sections.

2. Cut a piece of material, larger than the taped sections. Embellish the fabric with random flatlock seams (page 15).

3. Press the fabric to the back of the taped sections of fusible interfacing. Trim the excess material to the edges of the interfacing sections. Remove the tape.

4. Press another piece of material to the other side of the fusible interfacing. Trim the raw edges level with the interfacing.

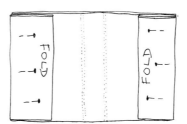

5. Cut two strips of fabric the same length as the book and 16 - 20 cm (**6 - 8"**) in width. Fold both strips in half making two strips 8 - 10 cm (**3 - 4"**) wide. (For small books reduce the width of these strips.)

6. Pin one strip to either end of the book cover. Align raw edges. These folded strips make the pockets for the book cover.

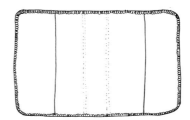

7. Using the same serger settings as described on page 47 sew round the outside edge. Trim the corners with the blade in a gentle arc. Chain off. Tidy the thread ends (page 13).

8. Slip the cover of the book into the pockets.

Random flatlock on book covers Jennie Rayment

Sewing Caddy

Travel is expensive

Always always read your itinerary. Always look at the little letters - I didn't. In 2006, I went to teach in Minnesota, travelled round a few places and ended up in Rochester. This was my last teaching venue. Had a most excellent day with my students before being transported to the airport. Happily, I waved goodbye to my driver then dragged my heavy bags into the small terminal. I had to find the United check-in desk - there wasn't one. Oh well, perhaps the flight is handled by another company - yes - on my ticket it said 'Mesa Airlines'. Mesa Airlines didn't have a desk either. I peered more closely at the ticket and it actually read 'Rochester n y'. Daylight dawned; n y wasn't part of the airport name like Washington Dulles but Rochester, New York! I was thousands of miles from the correct airport. An absolute absolute nightmare!

Cutting a long story short, I ended up purchasing a completely new ticket for the next day, flying via Minneapolis, Chicago, Detroit to Amsterdam and then back to Heathrow. As my original ticket proved to be totally non-refundable and I had to stay in a hotel for an extra night it was a very expensive mistake. But the most irritating part was flying over our house on the way to Amsterdam - why couldn't the pilot let me out?

Returning home from a northern quilt show also proved to be costly…….
After packing all the quilts, unsold books and patterns into the car, I tucked the purse containing a load of cash (for once had actually made a profit) into the driver's door pocket before going home. It was a five hour drive. The weather was appalling; heavy rain and swirling mist made the driving conditions on the motorway extremely heavy going. The journey got longer and longer. A 'comfort' stop became urgent; stopping at the next service station would be essential. Suddenly, the traffic came to a virtual standstill. Yard by yard, the cars crawled over the next few miles. Two hours later than expected, I arrived at the service station.

By now my physical situation was desperate. Flinging the car door open and with crossed legs (not once but twice), I hurtled into the loos, emerging a happier emptier woman.

Much later than intended, I arrived home. Wearily off-loaded the car before retrieving the cash from the door pocket. It was empty! All the money had gone; the purse had fallen out as I leapt out of the car. In my desperate state I just hadn't noticed.

Moral of this last sad tale: Never leave anything valuable in the door pocket of the car or do not drink before driving (what goes in has to come out).

Slightly frazzled cat - total failure to draw one with its legs crossed!

Sewing caddy

This ingenious case is ideal for holding small scissors, needles, pins, threads and thimbles whilst sat sitting hand-stitching in your favourite armchair. (Hand stitching? Yes even I have to do some things by hand, albeit only occasionally.) The caddy is simple to sew and quick to create. An ideal gift for all hand sewers.

Fabric choice

A medium weight cotton, firm silk, chintz or lightweight furnishing fabric with **no specific right or wrong side** would be a good choice.

Thread selection

Contrasting coloured threads to the chosen fabric emphasise the stitching. How about experimenting with some of the modern flosses and other textured threads for extra decorative embellishment on the upper and lower loopers**?**

You need:

30 x 115 cm (**12 x 45"**) fabric
50 x 30 cm (**20 x 12"**) fusible interfacing (see page 16/17)
Scraps of wadding/batting or other filling for a pincushion

From the 30 x 115 cm (**12 x 45"**) piece of fabric cut:

Sewing caddy front

Two 7.5 x 27 cm (**3 x 10½"**) strips + One 16.5 cm (**6½"**) square (scissors pocket)
One 25 x 16.5 cm (**10 x 6½"**) strip (second pocket) + One 27 x 13 cm (**10½" x 5"**) strip

Sewing Caddy back

Two 15 x 13 cm (**6 x 5"**) strips + One 23 x 16.5 cm (**9 x 6½"**) strip (pocket)

Pincushion & Base

One 15 x 13 cm (**6 x 5"**) strip (pincushion) + Two 7.5 x 13 cm (**3 x 5"**) strips (base)
Two 5 x 13 cm (**2 x 5"**) strips (connecting straps)

Fusible interfacing

One 27 x 13 cm (**10½ x 5"**) strip (caddy front)
One 15 x 13 cm (**6 x 5"**) strip (caddy back)
One 7.5 x 13 cm (**3 x 5"**) strip (pincushion base)

Serger Settings

Needles: Thread both or remove right-hand needle (page 10)
Blade: Disengage - or set at furthest distance from needle
Tensions: Regular
Stitch Length: Reduce to smaller stitch length
Stitch width: Variable - see text for details

Tip: Test the stitch appearance on a scrap of fabric and fusible interfacing before beginning.

Caddy front

1. Fold the 16.5 cm (**6½"**) square (scissors pocket) diagonally in half, R/S out, and press the crease firmly. Open out.

2. Lay the pressed square flat W/S up. Fold one corner inwards to touch the centre of the pressed crease, press in place.

3. Refold the square on the crease R/S out to form a triangle.

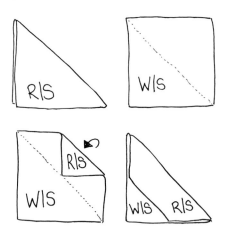

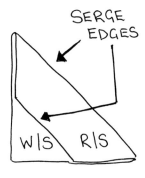

5. Fold the scissors pocket in half creating a smaller triangle. Make sure both sides of the folded edge are flush. Pin the layers together.

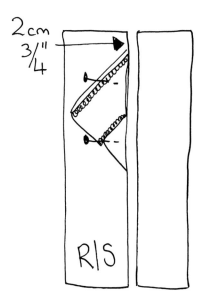

4. Reduce the stitch width (remove left-hand needle) and stitch length (page 12). Serge along both pressed diagonal folds of the scissors pocket.

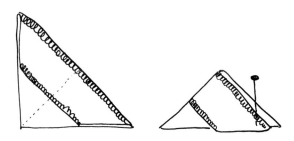

Tip: Insert all pins at right angles to the seam. (Less risk of the pins getting caught under the presser foot and/or in the mechanism.)

6. Place the pinned triangle on the R/S of one of the 7.5 x 27 cm (**3 x 10½"**) strips with the folded end approximately 2 cm (¾") from the start of the strip.

7. Lay the other 7.5 x 27 cm (**3 x 10½"**) strip on top, 'sandwiching' the pocket.

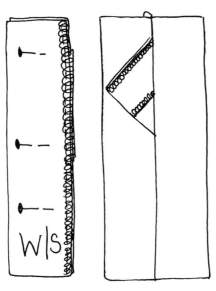

8. <u>Increase the stitch width to approximately 0.75 cm (¼").</u> <u>Insert right-hand needle.</u> Sew along the edge as shown in the diagram. Press the seam to one side. Leave the pocket flat.

9. Lay this section R/S up on the 27 x 13 cm **(10½ x 5")** fusible interfacing strip. Press in place and trim any excess material to the edges of the fusible interfacing.

10. Fuse the remaining 27 x 13 cm **(10½ x 5")** strip (R/S out) to the reverse of the fusible interfacing.

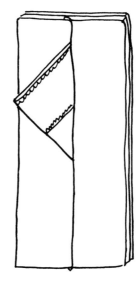

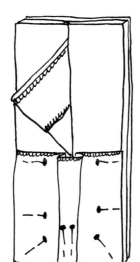

11. Prepare the second pocket:
Fold the 25 x 16.5 cm **(10 x 6½")** strip (R/S out) in half forming a 12.5 x 16.5 cm **(5 x 6½")** section. Embellish the folded edge with a narrow decorative stitch (see Stage 4).

12. Pin this pocket to the caddy front, aligning all the raw edges. Ease the excess material into a box pleat at the centre. Pin well.

13. <u>Reduce stitch length to minimum (remove left-hand needle).</u> Sew long sides first **then** sew the base of the pocket. **Leave top edge unsewn (above scissors pocket)**.

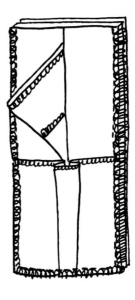

Pincushion

1. Fold the 15 x 13 cm (**6 x 5"**) strip in half (R/S out). Sew both long sides then stitch across one end.

2. Fill the pincushion with scraps of wadding/batting.

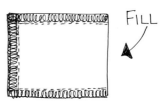

Tip: For a firm pincushion, fill it with sand. Line the inside of the pincushion with another layer of fabric. Stuff the end with small piece of wadding, add the sand then insert another small section of wadding to retain the sand in the pocket.

3. Pin both sides of the opening firmly together. Sew the raw edge.

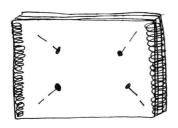

Pincushion base

1. Fuse one 7.5 x 13 cm (**3 x 5"**) strip to either side of the 7.5 x 13 cm (**3 x 5"**) fusible interfacing (pincushion base). All pieces are R/S out.

2. Sew the short sides **only**.

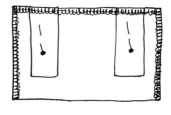

3. Fold both 5 x 13 cm (**2 x 5"**) strips in half widthways (R/S out). Serge edges. Cut both strips in half making four 2.5 x 6.5 cm (**1 x 2½"**) strips.

4. Pin two of the strips to either side of the pincushion base. Sew both the edges.

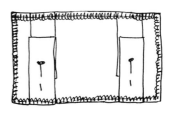

Caddy back

1. Fuse one 15 x 13 cm (**6" x 5"**) strip to either side of the 15 x 13 cm (**6 x 5"**) fusible interfacing section.

2. Make the pocket: Fold the 23 x 16.5 cm (**9 x 6½"**) strip in half (R/S out) forming an 11.5 x 16.5 cm (**4½ x 6½"**) section. Decorate the folded edge with a narrow stitch (Stage 4 Caddy Front).

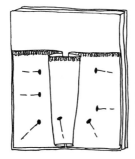

3. Pin the pocket to the caddy back, aligning all raw edges. Ease the excess material into a box pleat at the centre. Pin well (Stage 9 Caddy Front).

4. Sew the 15 cm (**6"**) sides first then stitch along the pocket bottom.

Assembling the caddy

1. Pin the straps of the pincushion base to unsewn side of the caddy front. Serge the edge.

2. Pin the other set of strips to unsewn side of caddy back and serge the raw edge.

Completing the caddy

Sorry, this has to be done by hand!

1. Open out the scissors pocket and secure the corners firmly with some small stitches. Why not add a bead or two to the corners of the pocket for extra embellishment?

2. Attach the pincushion to the base with a few firm stitches in all four corners. Again - think about a bead or small tassel for added embellishment.

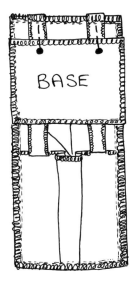

Finally.......... Fill the caddy with your small scissors, threads and other odds and bobs, select some sewing (preferably not mending) and relax in your favourite armchair. Never again will you have to dive down the sides of the chair to recover the pins, needles and reels of thread. Such luxury!

A thought......

Make the entire caddy much larger to hold a magazine, book or paper in the pockets. Increase the size of the scissors pocket to hold the television remote control. Two pockets could be made - an extra one for the DVD control. Ignore the pincushion and base and make the connecting straps longer.

Hang the caddy over <u>your</u> chair arm so that <u>you have access to the remote control</u>. Just think of the advantages - no more rapid changing of the programmes. Maybe you could watch your favourite show without anyone frantically zapping up and down through the television options. Bliss.

Sew up Sudoku

Be very careful what is packed in your carry-on baggage, as I was extremely embarrassed on one occasion...........

X-ray eyes

Left the house about 4.30 a.m. for the early flight to Aberdeen, all packed for a short teaching and lecturing trip. Hadn't had time before leaving the house for any personal titivating so I looked a middle-aged frump. My face lacked make-up, hair was a sad shade of mousy grey and I was attired in warm comfortable clothes with elasticated waistbands. A real fashion plate!

Arrived at Gatwick airport, checked in the luggage and bedecked with handbag, carry-on and a plastic bag or two with other vital travel impedimenta, set off for the departure lounge. Rush hour has begun and there is a long queue for security.

Have to admit, I had packed in a hurry slinging things in the cases willy-nilly, so my carry-on was crammed with assorted teaching and lecture paraphernalia. Passing safely through the metal detector, I turned to pick up my hand baggage. "Madame, you have something sharp in your carry-on!" "No, I haven't", I replied. (Almost certain that I had not flung any prohibited item in the case.) "I am sorry but I have to search your bag." "Please do," was my instant response - I like to be helpful.

He unzipped my bag. On the top, lay a large polythene bag filled with squares and other pieces of material; it was some of my lesson preparation. He removed the bag; underneath was a second bag very similar, followed by a third. I laughed and said, "I teach sewing." Clothing lay beneath the bags. Each piece was shaken, examined and laid out on the table in full view of the hordes of passengers jostling their way through security. First item was my black cape, followed by a little black bolero heavily embellished with Fancy Fandangoes in vivid colours, then my black skirt. This is a very brief garment - just a collection of short strips sewn together, there is not a lot of skirt!

By now, I had remembered what I had packed in my carry-on. Whoops.......The search continued. He removed my fishnet tights and my frilly black brassiere with large scarlet flowers and enormous red tassels. Then, he took out the black PVC thigh boots and under the boots was the whip! My black stock whip, ten feet long with a sturdy black leather wrapped handle and a red tipped end.

He looked up at this middle-aged frumpy now scarlet-faced woman, who repeated weakly, "I teach sewing you know!"

Sew up Sudoku

To reassure those who are wondering what the word Sudoku means, it is not some strange torture or odd kind of fabric but a number puzzle that is fast becoming an addictive craze across Britain. If you have never heard of it, read on.

6	3	2	5	4	1	7	9	8
8	7	5	2	3	9	1	4	6
9	1	4	8	6	7	3	5	2
1	9	3	7	5	8	6	2	4
4	2	8	9	1	6	5	3	7
5	6	7	4	2	3	9	8	1
2	4	9	6	7	5	8	1	3
3	5	6	1	8	4	2	7	9
7	8	1	3	9	2	4	6	5

Sudoku began in an American puzzle book about 1980 and was originally called 'Number Place'. Nicoli, a Japanese company that produced a range of pencil puzzles, spotted the puzzle. They introduced it to their readers in 1984 with the exotic title of "Suuji wa dokushin ni kagiru" but this lengthy title was shortened to Sudoku (Su means number and Doku means single).

In the early days the puzzle was not very successful but Nicoli made a few changes to the initial concept and created the format we see today. Now, Sudoku is the most popular number puzzle in Japan. It is very simple to learn, requires no calculations, and provides a surprisingly wide variety of logic situations. In addition it appeals to all ages.

3		2	1				4	
				3				
				7	4			9
5		8			3	7		
7		9				3		5
		1	7			2		4
2			4	8				
				5				
	6				7	1		3

Sudoku consists of nine blocks each containing nine squares. The numbers 1 - 9 are entered into the nine squares in each block and arranged in such a way that every line (top to bottom and side to side of the complete grid) also contains the numbers 1 - 9. Some of the numbers in the puzzle are given and you have to identify the others through reasoning and deduction.

According to one well known British television personality "It is an ideal puzzle for people who are not keen on crosswords and word games but love other games that stretch their minds," and she added, "...they don't need to be good at arithmetic!" Bliss!!

In reality, I think that the compiler of the first 'Number Place' puzzle was a patchwork and quilting devotee because the basis for the grid is a nine-patch.

Now relax, you don't have to complete a Suduko, there is one printed at the top of the page. It was the first one that my man solved - rated Moderate in the paper. It only took him three hours to figure out! Why not complete your own puzzle? Many of the British newspapers print a different Sudoku puzzle each day (the solution is in the next day's paper). For an easy life use the one shown here or the solution in the paper. However you obtain your completed Sudoku is irrelevant.

How to use the Suduko in a project?
Each number is represented by a colour:
1 = bright yellow, 2 = mid green, 3 = olive, 4 = brown, etc.

As everyone's selection of colours will be different, every design will be completely unique.

Colour choice
For good design definition, choose a variety of tints, tones and shades of different colours. (Tints are colours with white added, tones are colours with grey added and shades are colours with black added.) One more colour will be needed to frame the design - black is always a good option. For an overview of the completed project, crayon or paint a Sudoku in the relevant colours.

*Sudoku Tablecloth: 90 x 90 cm (**36 x 36"**)*
Medium-weight cotton sewn black bulk nylon thread

Big Sling Bag (page 21), **Wiggly Weaving tote & table mats** (page 98)

Wiggly Weaving with cover stitching

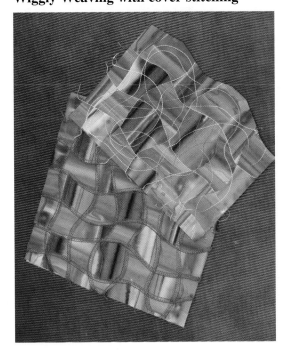

Crazy Log Cabin Cushion: 45 cm (18") (page 40)
Appliquéd 3D Four Petalled Flower (page 71)

**Crazy Log Cabin Quilt:
135 cm (53")**

Quilt features marbled fabric by Quilters
Treasure: www.QuiltersTreasure.com

Quickie Cushion & shopping bag: 40 cm (16") (page 37)

Square Caddy (page 51) **& Tissue Box** (page 32)

Octagonal Caddies (page 54)

Square Caddy (page 46), **Triangular and Hexagonal Caddies** (page 53)
Marbled fabric by Quilters Treasure: www.QuiltersTreasure.com

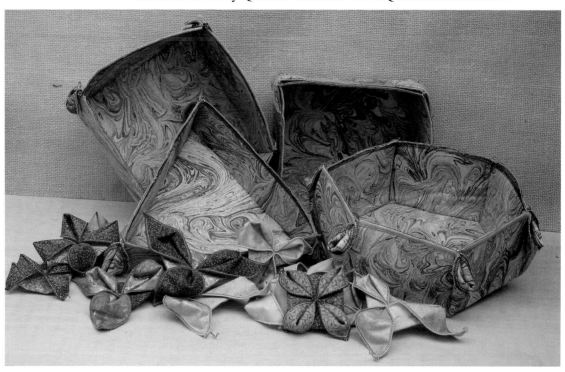

Square Caddy
(page 52) with appliquéd
3D flowers (page 71)

Big Sling Bag (page 21), **Wiggly Weaving** (page 98) **and book covers** (page 54)

Folded Quag (page 39): Quilt inside

Four Petalled Flowers (page 71)

Unfolded Quag:
Quilt embellished with buttons and quilting ties (page 42) plus Seaman Simon snoozing!

Sudoku tablecloth (page 65)

Sudoku tablecloth, woven mat (page 94) **and octagonal caddy** (page 54)

Square caddy (page 47), **Three and Four Petalled Flower Christmas decoration** (pages 71 & 75). Flowers pinned into polystyrene cone.

Crazy Log Cabin Rose: 56 cm (22")

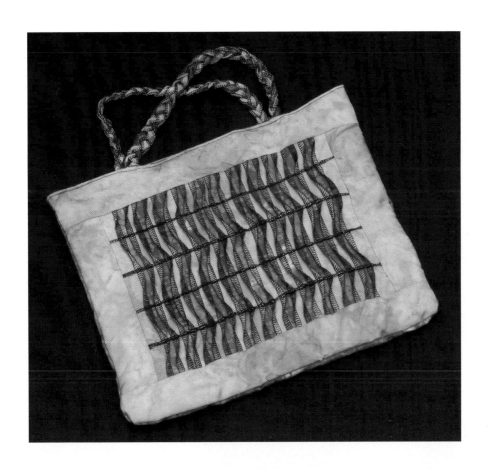

Tucked Totes: (page 79)
30 x 38 cm (12 x 15")
38 x 60 cm (15 x 24")

Tucked and twisted samples:
Black with metallic thread, two contrasting coloured strips stitched together and calico (muslin USA) as described on page 90 Stage b.

Tucked and piped cushion:
40 x 40 cm (16 x 16")
Tucks sewn with variegated thread (page 88).

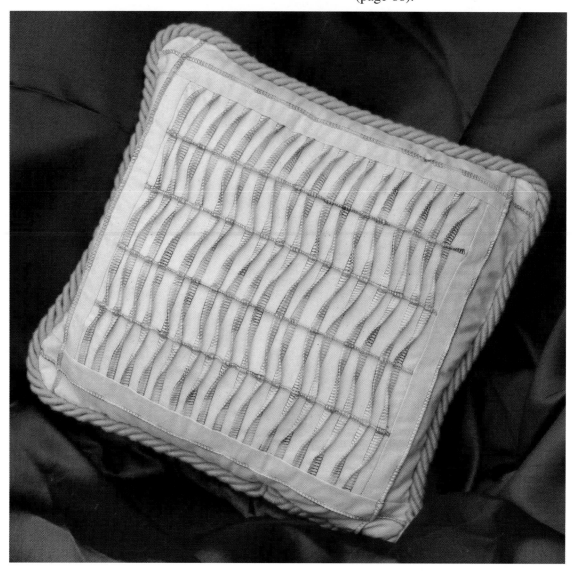

Tucked Cushion: (page 87)
38 x 30 cm (15 x 12")

Tucks sewn with variegated
thread by YLI Corp.

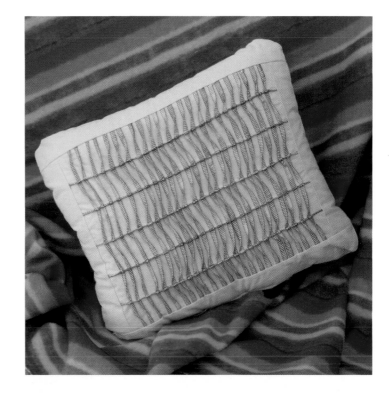

Tucked Cushions:
46 x 38 cm (18 x 15")
30 x 30 cm (12 x 12")

Embellished with Somerset
Patches (page 89)

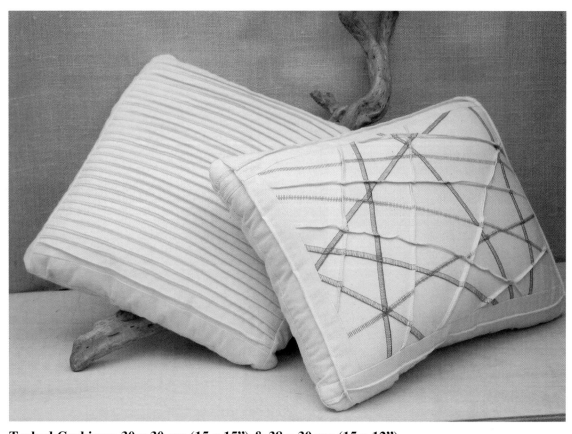

Tucked Cushions: 30 x 30 cm (15 x 15") & 38 x 30 cm (15 x 12")
Left-hand cushion features untwisted tucks, right-hand displays flatlock seams (page 91).

Tucked and piped cushion: 40 x 40 cm (16 x 16")
Tucks sewn in variegated thread (Robison-Anton Textile Co.) then twisted on diagonal (page 90).

Wiggly Woven Designs
Cushion: 38 x 38 cm (15 x 15") Embellished with cover stitching. Free motion sewing-machine quilting on cushion corners.

**Wiggly Woven
table mats and
Christmas card**
(page 98)

Wiggly Woven mats (page 98) **& Christmas table decoration:** (Polystyrene ring covered with 3D Flowers pinned in place.)

Woven mats (page 94)

More Ideas

Above: Totally Tucked: 117 x 137 cm (46 x 54")
Collage of assorted tucked panels embellished with
thread and yarn with appliquéd Tucked Circles.
Designs made on serger and sewing machine.

Left: Crossing Over Tucks and Trumpets (see
'Creative Tucks and Textures') embellished on
serger.

Tucked Circle: 70 x 70 cm (28 x 28")
(See 'Tucks and Textures Two'.)
Design sewn on serger. Machine applied and
quilted on sewing machine.

Scrip Bags
(For pattern see 'Tucks and Textures Two'.)
Left: Embellished with 3D Four petalled Flowers (page 71.
Right: Flap of bag created from Wiggly Weaving.

Scrip Bag
(For pattern see 'Tucks and Textures Two.')
Flap embellished with flatlock (page 15).

Woven mat (page 94)
Woven vase: Created from stiffened strips. Bit of a fiddle to create! Construction is similar to making a woven basket. Why not see if you can make one? Send me a picture when it is done.

www.jenrayment@aol.com.

Have fun!

Sudoku Tablecloth

Finished size: 90 x 90 cm **(36 x 36")**
(Alter the finished size of the cloth by increasing or decreasing the size of the squares.)

Fabric choice
Ensure that the fabric is washable. Pre-wash beforehand to prevent shrinkage and stop the colours bleeding (page 16). Spray starch the fabric after washing and before cutting to restore the 'body'.

Thread selection
The cloth in the photograph was sewn together using black bulk nylon to give a good coverage of the raw edges in addition to emphasising the grid structure of the design. Bulk nylon was threaded through both loopers and regular polyester through the needles.

You need
Width of all fabric metreage /yardage: 112/115 cm **(44/45")**
10 cm **(4")** fabric in nine different colours
20 cm **(8")** black fabric - first border
20 cm **(8")** fabric - second border
35 cm **(14")** fabric - outer border

Serger Settings: Regular

Needles: Both needles threaded
Blade: Engaged
Tensions: Regular
Stitch Length: Reduce to slightly smaller stitch length
Stitch width: Reduce stitch width to 0.65 cm (¼") by altering stitch finger position - retract or remove entirely (page 12).

1. Decide on which colour of fabric is to represent each number. Cut a scrap from each colour and label with the relevant number, as it is easy to forget.

2. Cut nine 9 cm (3½") squares from each colour. Numbering the R/S of each square with an adhesive label, scrap of masking tape or water-soluble pen, will help when arranging the design. (Underline 6 and 9 to prevent confusion!)

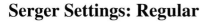

6	3	2	5	4	1	7	9	8
8	7	5	2	3	9	1	4	6
9	1	4	8	6	7	3	5	2
1	9	3	7	5	8	6	2	4
4	2	8	9	1	6	5	3	7
5	6	7	4	2	3	9	8	1
2	4	9	6	7	5	8	1	3
3	5	6	1	8	4	2	7	9
7	8	1	3	9	2	4	6	5

3. Sudoku is conveniently divided by a heavy grid into nine blocks. Arrange nine fabric squares **in the correct order** to form one of the blocks.

4. Sew these squares together as shown in the diagram below. Use 0.65 cm (¼") seam allowance or thereabouts. (See page 12.) The seam allowance selected is not critical but **must be consistent**. As the seams are on the right-side of the cloth, remember to stitch the pieces with W/Ss together. Watch the blade carefully - only the whiskers are being removed from the fabric edges not great chunks!

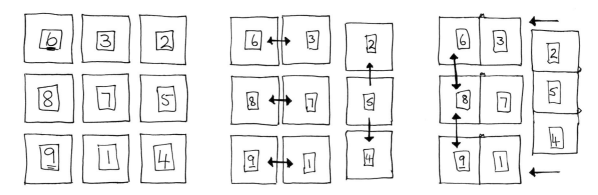

5. Construct the other eight blocks in the same fashion. ***Keep checking that the colours are in the correct places*** - unpicking serged/overlocked seams wastes yards of thread and takes blooming ages.

6. Join all nine blocks together as in Stage 4 above. **Watch the pattern arrangement carefully**. Remove labels and press well.

7. Cut 4 cm (**1½"**) wide strips in black for the first border.

Advice on adding a border
Measure opposite sides. Cut two strips this length x required width. (The width of the border is your choice - do remember to add the seam allowances before you cut.) Stitch one strip to each side. Open the strips out and measure the remaining edges (from top and bottom) of the panel. Cut two more strips to this measurement. Sew in place.

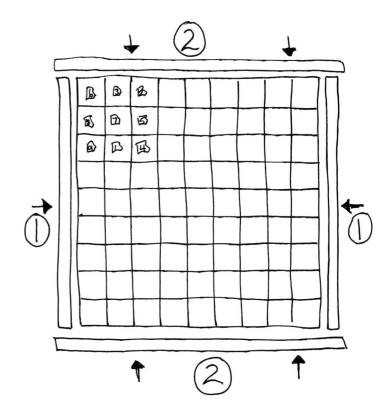

Sew the border strips to the centre panel. Press carefully.

8. Second border: Measure the sides. Cut 3 cm (**1¼"**) strips the correct length and desired width. Sew on to the panel.

9. Cut four 8.5 cm (**3¼"**) strips x 100 cm (**39"**) approximately for the outer border. Before attaching to the tablecloth, embellish the middle of the strips with a decorative flatlock.

Serger Settings: Flatlock

Needles: Remove right-hand needle. Tape thread to top of machine
Blade: Disengage
Tensions: Loosen left-hand needle tension - turn to lowest number
      Tighten lower looper - turn to highest number
Stitch Length: Reduce to smaller stitch length
Stitch width: Widest. Set stitch finger at maximum (page 12)

Take one strip and fold one third over (R/S together). Sew along the fold. Pull the strip flat (it may need a firm tug to become totally flat). Repeat with the other strips.

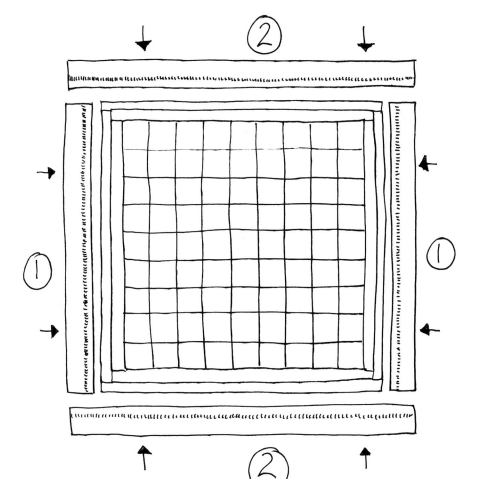

Sew the strips to the sides of the cloth with the flatlocked seam towards the centre.

Attach one strip to each of the opposite sides. Trim the raw edges level with the cloth. Attach the other two strips to the remaining sides. Trim raw edges level.

10. Sew round the outside edge of the cloth. Reduce the stitch width or set the machine for a rolled hem.

Serger Settings: Rolled Hem

Needles: Remove left-hand needle. Tape spare thread to top of machine
Blade: Engage
Tensions: Right-hand needle as normal
Tighten lower looper - turn to higher number
Stitch Length: Regular
Stitch Width: Narrow - retract stitch finger (page 12)

Draw an arc in each corner before you commence sewing. Rounded corners are much easier to sew along the edge in one continuous line - no corners to jiggle round. Use a plate or any round object as a template to keep all the arcs a similar shape.

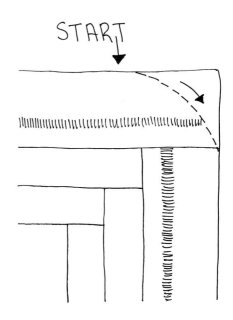

Start the stitching just before the arc. Sew round the arc following the drawn line, trimming the fabric with the cutting blade. Trim the other three corners in the same fashion. On completion of the sewing, chain off and tidy thread ends (page 13).

11. Press the cloth well. Lay it on the table and admire!

Other ideas

a. Make a reversible table cloth: Use materials with no discernible right or wrong side - plains or batiks would be an excellent choice.

b. Turn the design into a cot quilt: Mount the panel on wadding/batting. Add a backing fabric. Secure the layers with a few quilting ties (page 42).

c. Create a 230 cm (**90"**) square duvet cover: Cut 24 cm (**9½"**) squares. Add a 9 cm (**4½"**) border to all the sides.. Cut backing fabric to fit. Pin the two layers together. Stitch three sides. Add Velcro or some duvet tape (with poppers attached) or buttons to the remaining side.

d. For a double bed quilt - cut 23 cm (**9"**) squares. Add a 10 cm (**4½"**) border. Mount onto wadding and a backing fabric. Quilt the layers together by hand or on the sewing machine. Bind the raw edge. Makes a 220 cm (**87"**) square approximately.

e. Complete your table linen with a few napkins or serviettes - call them what you will. It depends on how 'proper' you wish to speak! Cut 40 - 50 cm (**16 - 20"**) squares of fabric. Follow Stage 10: Draw a gentle arc on each corner. Set the serger for a rolled hem and sew round the raw edge.

Three D Flowers

Champagne before lunch!
Never ever feed me champagne on an empty stomach, as the consequences may be dire.

Early days of my fourth relationship (oh yes, I am working on man number four), I was escorted to a very posh society wedding in a Guild Hall in London. It was an extraordinarily up-market and a really proper 'do'.

A lengthy church service was followed by a very long reception with copious quantities of champagne and minimalistic nibbles. I sank rapidly. The influence of the wine and the effort of being exquisitely well behaved in addition to making charming small talk to many unknown family guests proved most arduous. Eventually, we were summoned to the Dining Hall. To my horror, all the guests had pre-designated places with their names in elegant copper-plate handwriting on a card beside the individual plates. Nightmare - I was not seated next to my man! My name was on the other side of an enormous table. A swathe of white napery separated us.

Surreptitiously, I tried to change the names over. Got caught in the act by one of the other guests. She told me very firmly to remain in my appointed spot. Chastened, I sat. An extremely nice looking gentleman sat down and seeing I was visibly upset, inquired most pleasantly who I was and what did I do? I replied "I am Jennie Rayment and I am that man's mistress!" and I pointed to my man across the table. Silence fell.

Many months later, still with the same guy, we were having a late lunch in an exceedingly swanky hotel bar full of upper class bods with cut glass accents. It was the kind of place where the twin-set and pearl brigade and a handful of 'Hooray Henrys' rule sublime. Gentility at its best! Champagne for various reasons was consumed before the food arrived. Do you know that hotel had the temerity to deliver lukewarm soup, no condiments were offered and much much more worser ....they put butter on the bread of my smoked salmon sandwiches. Really! How disgusting! Were the hotel kitchen staff complete idiots? Did they not appreciate I only eat smoked salmon on plain thinly sliced brown bread? Did I let everyone within earshot know? Yes. I could hear myself sounding forth at great length. Could I stop the flow of verbal garbage? No. It is those little bubbles in the wine that cause all the trouble, or so I like to believe!

This inability to retain my drink in a sombre and sensible fashion goes to back to my childhood. I was christened at 18 months old or thereabouts. At the celebration tea following the church service, I tottered round the guests as they toasted me with champagne. Several people left their semi-full glasses on the low tables and unbeknown to everyone, I consumed the contents. Some time later, was found sitting in a cardboard box singing quietly to myself. According to my mother, this was not dissimilar behaviour to my grandmother after someone inadvertently gave this 90 year old lady a large glass of very potent malt whisky. I have to confess that history does not relate if she was found sitting in a cardboard box as well.

Three D flowers

Fast, fun and very easy to make. These flowers can be used for decorative embellishment on garments, quilts and soft furnishings, made into festive wreaths and even used as a pin or brooch. The good news ......They are most excellent for covering any little glitch in the seam or concealing any dodgy stitching on your work. The bad news............. A small amount of hand sewing is needed in the construction.

Choose to construct either four or three petalled flowers or make several of each.

For a more interesting appearance, combine two different coloured materials. Both types of flowers can be made any size and from most light or medium-weight materials. Why not try striped material for really jazzy flowers - the stripes will all go in different directions? Alternatively make them out of gauze, voile and net and other sheer fabrics.

Chaining off at the end of each seam and leaving the thread ends hanging freely adds further ornamentation to the petal tips.

You need
Two 15 cm (**6"**) squares of fabric in two different colours

Serger Settings: Rolled Hem

Needle: Remove left needle
Blade: Engaged - set at normal
Tensions: Tighten lower looper - 7/9
Stitch Length: Reduce to smaller stitch length
Stitch width: Retract stitch finger - use narrow stitch width (page 12)

Four-petalled flowers

1. Draw a 13 cm (**5"**) square on <u>R/S</u> of one of the fabrics. Draw the square in the middle leaving 1cm (½") seam allowance outside the drawn line.

Tip: Make a 13 cm (5") square template from a piece of card or draw round one of the square Perspex rulers used with rotary cutters.

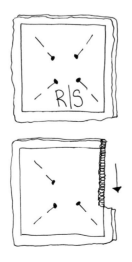

2. Lay the first piece of fabric on the second, drawn side up, <u>W/Ss together</u>. Pin both layers together (insert pins inside the drawn line to prevent them catching in the blade).

3. Sew along one side of the square following the pencil line, trimming the excess material with the blade. Chain off at end of seam. Do not trim the thread ends.

4. Repeat on the remaining three sides. Press well. Pull the loose thread ends to lock the stitching. Trim the excess thread leaving a short tail approximately 2 cm (¾") in length.

5. Press the square in half and half again to mark the centre.

6. Lay the pressed square on a flat surface. Fold the opposite sides to the middle of the square - the opposite sides should touch exactly on the crease. At the centre of the square, sew all the layers firmly together.

As this stitching will be visible in the finished flower, choose a thread colour that tones with the fabric. The sewing can be done by hand (Hmmmmmmm!) or on a sewing machine. For those who choose the machine method, select a short stitch length and stitch forwards and backwards across the junction.

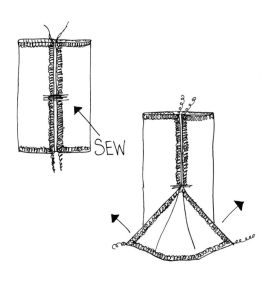

7. Turn the fabric lengthways and pull out the two corners. Pull back the corners until the third side of the square can be brought to touch the centre stitching.

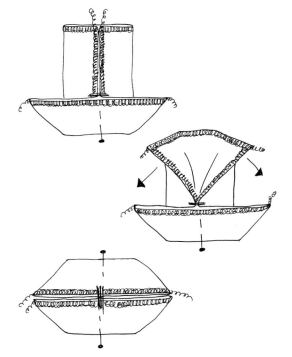

A 'boat' shape is formed. Pin in place.

8. Repeat at the other end making a second boat shape.

9. By hand, sew both edges to the centre (on the crease). Sew through all the layers. If preferred, use the sewing machine as in Stage 6.

For diagramatic clarity, the serged stitching on the edge of the material is not shown in the next few sketches.

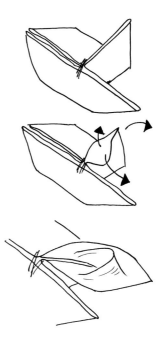

10. Lift one of the 'ears' and turn back - as arranging the collar on a garment. A petal shape is formed. Repeat the same action with the other three ears.

This Four-petalled flower can be sewn in place with a few small stitches along the base of the flower or in the centre of the petals. The petals can be secured at the tip if necessary.

Ideas for Play

a. Cut different sized squares. Place one flower on top of another.

b. Stitch a bead in the centre of the flower.

c. Make two small flowers in silk, sew together and create a decorative pin or brooch.

d. Cut the flower square on the bias: the petal edges are more flexible than the petals from a straight cut square BUT cutting on the bias requires more fabric.

e. Make the flowers from one layer of material not two. Select a material with no discernible right or wrong side, as the W/S will show.

f. Trim thread ends to the fabric, secure with either fray check or tie off (page 13).

g. Save material by rotary cutting the squares to the exact measurement. The rolled edge may not be quite as neat and if your hand wobbles a bit, the blade might trim more one side than the others. Should this happen then sew round again, trimming the other sides by the same amount!

Three-petalled flowers

1. Trace or photocopy one of the triangle templates (page 103). Cut out the template. Draw round the template on a piece of fabric. Cut out roughly, leaving a small seam allowance outside drawn line.

2. Follow Stages 2 - 4 page 70.

3. Press the triangle in half from point to centre of opposite side. Repeat on the other two points. The three pressed lines will intersect at centre of triangle (with a bit of luck!).

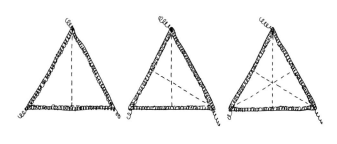

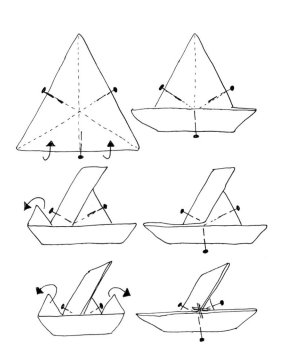

4. Lay the triangle on a flat surface. Mark the middle of all three sides (on pressed crease) with a pin.

5. Fold up one side of the triangle evenly and parallel to the outer edge, matching middle of side to the centre mark (where the pressed creases cross). Press, and pin in place after removing marker pin.

6. Repeat with the next side: Fold the side evenly and parallel to the outside edge. Pin in place. Pull out the corner/flap.

7. Finally, bring the last side to the centre, folding evenly and parallel to the outside edge etc. Open out both corners/flaps. Pin in place. Press.

All midpoints of the three sides now touch at the central point of the triangle.

8. Stitch across this junction (see next paragraph), carefully anchoring all the points together. Sew through all the layers.

By hand: start on the W/S in the centre, bring needle up through layers catching the edge of **each** fold with a **small** stitch - secure each section individually. Add a bead or button at the same time.

By sewing machine: use a very short stitch length, sew the edges of the folds in place where they touch at the centre with the minimum number of stitches. For speed: attach the darning/hopper foot, lower feed dogs, set stitch width and length settings to zero; sew a few stitches in a sort of 'Y' or 'T' shape to catch all three folds together at the centre.

9. Finally, lift one 'ear' up; pull sides apart and open out, fold tip back and away from centre. Arrange to make a petal shape. Repeat with the other two 'ears' to make three petals.

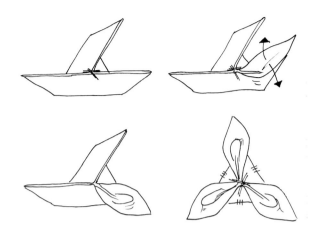

Attach the Three-petalled flower anywhere you fancy by simply sewing through the centre and along the sides. Why not add a bead at this stage?

Playtime

a. Create decorations for a festive table: pin flowers into a polystyrene ring for a seasonal wreath or a candle holder (don't let the flowers catch fire!) for a gala occasion. Stack a few flowers on a barbecue stick or small knitting needle to resemble a miniature tree.

b. Sew two flowers together to make a six petalled shape. How about a smaller one on top of a larger one? Create a really innovative decoration: make two small ones and one larger one, sew one smaller one to the front of the larger one, sew the remaining small flower on the back, suspend with a fine thread.

c. Add sequins to the tips, and how about a tassel or two? Attach a couple of Three-petalled flowers to the chest area with a tassel apiece could be a show-stopper; add small beads to the tassels ends and make 'em twirl. The mind boggles!

Make an iris
This way of folding the
Three-petalled Flower
makes a delightful shape
similar to an iris.

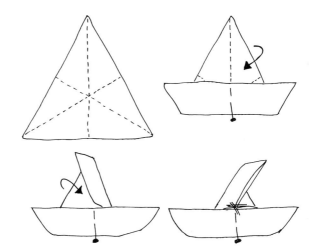

1. Follow Stages 1 - 4
page 74, but insert a pin
in the centre of only one
of the sides. Fold this
side further than the
centre of the triangle
(beyond the junction of
the three creases).

2. Bring the other two
sides to touch the pin.

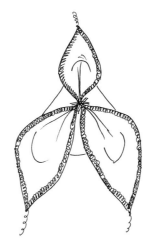

3. Stitch across the junction of
the three sides.

4. Fold back the ears as in the
previous flower - there will be
one small petal and two larger
ones - just like an iris.
Well……..almost!

Tucked Totes

Jennie Rayment - TV star!
A year or so ago, I received an invitation to make yet another television show with Alex Anderson. She hosts 'Simply Quilts', an American show produced by HGTV. The studio rang in mid-December and told me that the show would be shot in early January in Los Angeles.

Panic-struck - I had less than three weeks to prepare and what was I going to demonstrate? The sunflower design from '**Creative Tucks and Textures**' would be brilliant, lots of twiddles and easy to explain. The production team recommended making several stage samples of each part of the technique in case any section of the show had to be re-shot. This would save frantically unpicking any mistakes that I made whilst demonstrating the construction. The studio requested a small quilt featuring the sunflower plus a larger version exhibiting design development. Christmas would be very busy that year.

By 11th January, the samples were made, the quilts completed, the bags packed with all the stuff for the studio and it was time to go. Sneezing madly and full of cold, I set off for the airport - only twelve hours travelling and I would be in Los Angeles. Checked into my hotel, coughed somewhat at the cost of the room as well as from my cold. Finally collapsed snuffling and sniffling on a most luxurious bed (maybe the hotel was worth that vast amount of dollars). By 3.30 a.m., I was wide-awake, the delights of jet lag! As it was an early start at the studio, I got up and began to get ready for my performance.

Shower and hair wash was the first task, so smothered myself with all the little bottles of freebie shampoos and lotions. Nails next - nail polish was de rigeur (a real shock to the system) and it had to be a pale waffy colour not a lurid pink. Whilst painting my nails, I glanced in the mirror and had a real shock - my face and neck were covered in a bright red rash. Was it the shampoos, nerves or some other allergy? Glory be - what would I look like under the arc lamps of the studio? My nose was already red from the cold, I was aware that my voice was getting huskier and now my face was like a beetroot. My delusions of grandeur ....'Jennie Rayment - TV star of Twiddling and Fiddling'... were rapidly shrinking. Yet another nightmare!

By 7.00 a.m., had packed and was waiting in the lobby for the cab. My face was still brilliant red with the rash and my nose streamed even more. As I humped my bags into the cab, most of my right thumbnail ripped off. Now I had a bright pink face, no thumbnail and incipient flu. A really good beginning!

Five minutes later, the cab arrived at the studio............. Each segment of the show was carefully rehearsed and rehearsed and rehearsed so many times that I began to feel numb and most distinctly brain dead. Alex Anderson whizzed past several times in various states of readiness for the show - she got more glamorous each time she passed. The wardrobe department accepted my outfit. Thank goodness, I had made my waistcoat especially for the show - have to strut your stuff! The Makeup girl beckoned, settled me before the mirror surrounded by all those light bulbs. Oh so Hollywood. She swooshed a white fluffy powder puff over my cheeks then completed my makeup with a enormous amount of bright red lipstick and outlined my lips with a thick dark line. She super-glued my broken thumb nail in place with an inordinately large amount of adhesive - would I stick to everything else? Staring at my somewhat lurid visage in the mirror I saw that the rash had gone. I only had a bright red nose, a white face, and a garish gash for a mouth, a rapidly deepening throaty voice and a large globule of glue on my thumbnail. Maybe the US viewers would think this was normal for middle-aged British ladies?

At 11.30, the show began. There was a quick run-through with the director, lighting guy and other bods to show the sequence of all the stage samples. Everything was carefully arranged so that the camera lens could focus and frame the pieces correctly. Hands had to be moved carefully so the sample on display was not obscured. If anything was handled, it was important to remember to hold it flat and offer it up towards the camera, in the meantime keeping your fingers out of the way. Needless to say there are many shots of a large thumbnail embellished with super glue!

Once the quick rehearsal over - it was for real. Cameras rolled and the lights went up and we were on! Nerve-wracking! Whatever happens in your demonstration - good or bad (within reason) is transmitted. You can't stop and say, "Please can we do that again" or collapse in despair or giggles because you have said something completely erroneous or very stupid. Parts of the show cannot be shot repeatedly as you see on TV out-takes programmes. This is for real! I mentally crossed my fingers and hoped I would not make a real fool of myself. Each segment had to be carefully timed and because the third section was too short it had to be shot again, and then they stopped it halfway. "Start again" commanded the director "from your centre sample. Keep the energy and the interest going!" Try starting off in the middle of a demo (hoping you remembered the sequence of words) and sounding all excited and energetic at the same time.

An hour or so later, it was over. Warts and all, **"Creative Tucks and Textures"** was in the can. I had done it and could go. Alex had three more shows to do that day. It is not a very relaxing time for her, as forty-plus shows will be shot in two weeks - all different tutors and techniques. The life of a TV presenter is not as easy as she makes it look.

Daisy Delight
66 cm (26") square
As featured on
Simply Quilts.

Pattern available
(See inside back cover)

Tucked totes

These days, most people appear to be festooned with a variety of holdalls from bags, pouches, reticules to totes; they are a most necessary part of daily life. Why not make a 'designer' one with a textured dimension? Here is an easy bag to make with an interesting textured panel of tucks and a plaited handle.

Thread selection

Select threads that match or provide a contrast to the material colours. The strips in the pink and orange bag were sewn with black thread through the loopers and both needles. (For economy, buy large reels of serger thread - sergers/overlockers consume enormous quantities.) For good definition of the tuck edges and the grid structure, a contrasting thread to the fabric colours is advisable.

The blue and white stripy tote (back cover and below) was sewn with three threads - variegated bulk (woolly) nylon on the upper looper, black polyester on the lower looper and cream through the left-hand needle (right needle removed).

Tip: Test the stitching to check the thread tensions (page 11). Bulk nylon usually requires less tension than the regular setting; turn the dial to a lower number.

Fabric choice

Any medium weight cotton dressmaking/patchwork fabric or a light weight furnishing material would be ideal. Pre-washing the fabric is advisable. Press carefully, applying a light coating of spray starch. Crisp materials are much easier to fold and manipulate - they hold the creases well.

You need

50 cm (**20"**) approximately (min 112 cm/**44"** wide) of <u>two different fabrics</u>
(Total metreage/yardage depends on the finished size of the bag).
50 cm (**20"**) approximately (min 112 cm/**44"** wide) wadding/batting*
Firm low-loft cotton or wool wadding is preferable to polyester. (Polyester may stretch.)

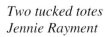

Two tucked totes
Jennie Rayment

1. From the first fabric: Cut <u>four</u> 2.5 x 112 cm (**1 x 44"**) strips. Cut across the material from selvedge to selvedge.

2. From the second fabric: Cut <u>five</u> 2.5 cm (**1"**) wide strips. Cut across the material from selvedge to selvedge.

Serger Settings

Needles: Thread both. (Remove right needle if using three threads - page 10)
Blade: Engaged
Tensions: Regular
Stitch Length: Normal
Stitch width: Reduce to 0.65 cm (¼") by altering stitch finger position - retract slightly or remove entirely (page 12)

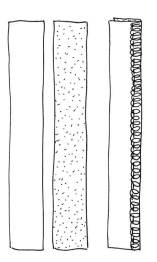

3. Check the thread tension and test the stitching.

4. Sew the strips in pairs (R/S out), one strip from each colour. Stitch a 0.65 cm (¼") seam or thereabouts. An <u>even</u> seam width is more important than an exact 0.65 cm/¼". Ensure the same coloured strip is on top each time - be consistent. Watch the blade carefully; the whiskers are trimmed from the fabric edges and nothing more.

Tip: Don't chain off at the seam end - place the next set of strips under the presser foot and keep sewing. Saves a lot of thread.

5. Gently press all the pairs of strips flat. Press the seam on to the same colour each time.

6. Join the pairs of strips together to make a wide band. Watch carefully, don't catch the first seams in the next ones. Unpicking is a pain!

Tip: Check the stitching occasionally, gremlins alter the tension when you are not looking. :o)

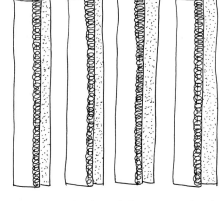

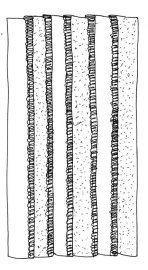

7. Gently press the band flat. Press both sides of the strip, pressing all the seams in the same direction.

Cut the strip to size
For a short tucked panel, cut 27 cm (**10½"**) lengths. For a longer panel, cut 37 cm (**14½"**) lengths.

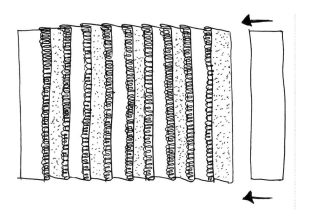

1. Join these lengths together making a wide band. The width of the band is your choice.

From the remaining 2.5 cm (**1"**) strip, cut the same length as the sewn band. Attach this to one of the sides to balance the colour arrangement of the strips. The same colour is now at both ends of the band.

2. Press band well on both sides turning all the tucks in the same direction.

3. Measure 6 cm (**2¼"**) from the top of the panel and rule a line. Rule more lines at 5 cm (**2"**) intervals across the panel leaving a 6 cm (**2¼"**)section at the bottom.

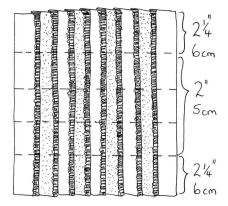

Serger Settings

Needles: Remove left needle
Blade: Disengage
Tensions: Regular
Stitch Length: Normal
Stitch width: Narrow. Retract stitch finger completely

4. Fold the fabric on the first ruled line and sew across the tucks. It is much easier to position the material with all the pressed tucks facing you. You are then going with the flow!

5. Turn the work, fold the fabric on the next set of marks and sew across the tucks, twisting them all in the opposite direction. (Flip them over, reverse the twist - your choice of words.)

6. Repeat on every line - alternating the direction of the tucks as you sew.

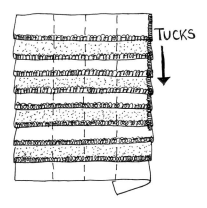

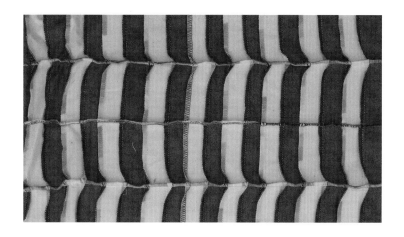

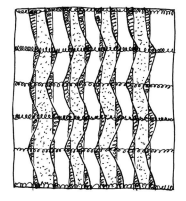

On the outer edges, secure the tucks with a narrow line of stitch. Complete the twisted design by turning the tucks in the reverse direction to the adjacent line of stitch. Sew close to the raw edges.

Adding the border
The borders of the tucked panel can be any width you like. Decide on a suitable measurement.

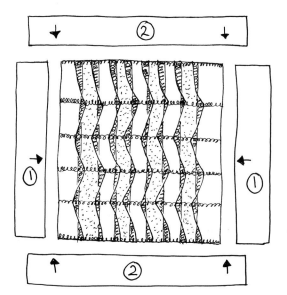

1. Cut two strips the exact length of the tucked panel. Attach to opposite sides.

2. Measure the width of the tucked panel - pull it gently to get the true measurement. Cut two strips this length. Pin both ends of the strip to the panel. Sew in place.

Tip: Remember to insert pins at right angles to the seam.

3. Press the borders carefully, pressing all the seams towards the outside edge.

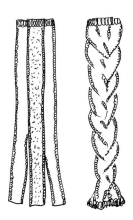

Making the handles
1. Cut four 2 cm (¾") wide strips from selvedge to selvedge (full width of fabric 115 cm **44/45"**) from one of the material. In addition, cut two 2 cm (¾") wide strips from the other material.

2. Take <u>two strips of the same colour</u>. Place W/Ss together. Serge both sides of the strip. Repeat with the remaining strips making three 115 cm **44/45"**) serged strips.

3. Cut all three strips in half - making six lengths approximately 55 cm (**22"**) long. Pin three of these lengths together - two of one colour and one of the other.

4. Plait these three lengths together.

Tip: Put the pinned end of the band underneath the presser foot. Lower the presser foot onto the band to hold it firmly whilst you plait.

When the plaiting is complete, pin the three strips together. Serge across the end of the plait to secure the strips. Repeat with the remaining three lengths to form a second plait.

Constructing the Tote

1. Measure the size of the completed bordered panel and cut three more pieces of fabric to this size. (Two pieces are for the bag lining and <u>the third is for the back of the bag</u>.)

2. Cut two pieces of wadding/batting slightly larger than the completed bordered panel.

3. Lay the panel on one piece of wadding. Pin the layers well. Increase the stitch length to maximum. Keep the seam allowance 0.65 cm (¼").

Sew round the raw edge of the panel, trimming the excess wadding with the blade.

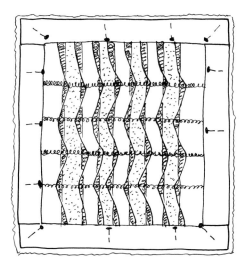

4. Lay the back of bag section of material on the second piece of wadding. Pin the layers well. Serge the raw edges as in Stage 3.

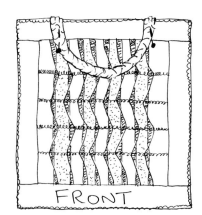

5. Pin a handle to each half of the bag - be careful to pin handles at the same spacing on both sides of bag.

6. Pin one piece of lining to one end of each half of the bag, R/Ss together. Sew in place. Shorten the stitch length as you sew over the handles. Leave the pins in place. Trim the handle ends flush with the edge of the lining.

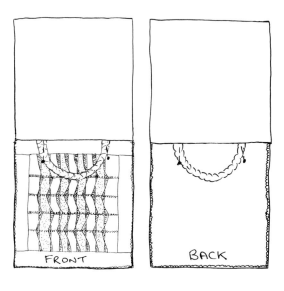

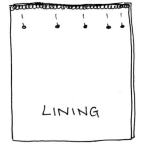

7. Open out both halves of the bag. Place one half on top of the other. Pin the layers well.

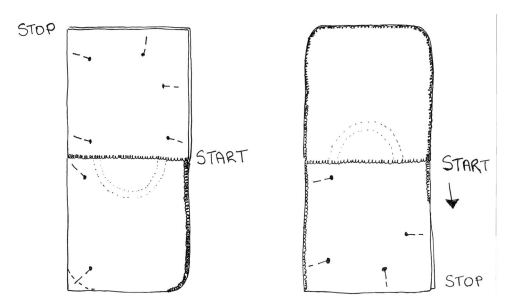

8. Draw arcs on the lower corners of the bag, as shown above. Start the stitching at the seam between the lining and the front of the tote. Sew round the bag, trimming the corners with the blade. Continue stitching until the bottom of the lining is reached (left drawing).

9. Flip the bag over and sew from the start of the first seam to the end of the lining (right drawing above).

10. Turn the bag through the gap in the lining.

11. Close the gap with a line of stitch. Use a wide seam allowance and trim about 2 cm (¾") from edge of lining. (Trimming a small amount off the base of the lining ensures that it fits nicely inside the bag.)

12. Press the top of the bag lightly.

Finally...........

To keep the lining neatly inside the bag, fold the handles into the bag and sew the top edge with a narrow seam. (Reduce seam width by removing left-hand needle.)

Ideas for design development
a. For a subtly different tucked effect, cut wider strips.

b. Make the spacing between the parallel lines of stitch across the tucks wider.

c. Use the technique as a textured panel for a cushion front, quilt block or small cot quilt.

d. Experiment with different sized strips and a variety of threads, (if you can be bothered to re-thread the serger!!) then twist the tucks at random intervals.

e. For longer handles, cut longer strips or join strips together. Any seams in the fabric will get lost in the plaiting.

Tucks and Twists

Waving the flag

Just before Quilt Festival, a highly prestigious quilt event staged each autumn in Houston, Texas, opens to the public, there is an event called the Wearables Walkabout Luncheon. This is a fashion show with food. The audience sit enjoying a good lunch while models strut about on a small catwalk displaying a series of garments and accessories. Near by, a speaker expounds the amazing attributes of each artefact.

I have modelled on several occasions sporting a selection of my nipped, tucked, twiddled and fiddled muslin (referred to as calico in UK) garments. One year, I appeared as the 'Muslin Mistress' and Angela Madden (internationally known British quilter) was press-ganged into being the presenter. She told the audience the tale of the Muslin Mistress going to meet her lover. While she related the story and pontificated on the fascinating qualities of my garments, I slowly removed most of the clothes. Off came the cloak, the brolly was discarded, the naughty nightie was ripped off (thank goodness for Velcro) revealing a camisole embellished with tassels and a frilly pair of muslin knickers/bloomers (call then what you will). Do not worry dear reader, despite being semi-clothed, nothing untoward was exposed. As I stood on the catwalk, Angela said, "Being a Muslin Mistress is very boring due to all the time spent flat on her back. But this outfit has one great advantage, as she lies there, the Muslin Mistress can always think of Britain." Where upon, I turned to reveal a large Union flag sewn on the back of my muslin bloomers.

The flag had been a last minute idea and had been constructed rapidly using a form of reverse appliqué. On completion, it was cobbled speedily to the back of the underwear. Little did I know that I had made a grave mistake. I had got the Union flag design back to front. No one told me displaying the flag this way round is a signal of distress.

This outfit has been worn at many lectures all over the world since that auspicious occasion and I was very sad when I mislaid the knickers somewhere in England. Weeks passed and I searched everywhere. It was most unfortunate because I really did not want to have to make another pair. To my great delight, the phone rang one day and a gentleman asked if I possessed a pair of bloomers with a flag on the back. "Yes, I do or rather I did." "Well", he replied, "I have just found a pair behind the waste bin in the Ladies loo and one of the staff said that they probably belong to you."

My knickers had been found in a church hall in Kidderminster. They must have fallen behind the bin when I changed.

I suspect the caretaker was a trifle puzzled at their discovery - not exactly the most common item to find in an ecclesiastical building. I didn't discuss the reason for the flag!

Tucks and twists

Making panels of tucks has appeared in some of my other books. The tucks were sewn on the sewing machine then twisted in different directions to form a pattern. In '**Creative Tucks and Textures**' the text also explains how to embellish the edge of the tucks for a really superduper extra creatively snazzy design.

Now......The serger can not only make a tuck but also embellish the edge at the same time. It is able to multi-task just like a woman! (Yes, I know this can be done on a sewing machine but the serger is faster. I don't do slow if I can help it.)

Inaccurate stitching does not always matter when making some tucked designs. The reflection of light from an uneven surface hides a multitude of sins, consequently if the odd tuck goes slightly awry it will not be noticed as minor aberrations are concealed in the textured surface. Mistakes do not matter - the result is just a little different.

Fabric choice
A crisply finished, medium-weight material in a plain colour or a simple self-patterned print is ideal. Cottons, silks and other natural fibres are preferable to man-made fibres such as polycotton which has too much 'spring' in it.. Heavily decorated or large multicolored designs tend to obscure the textured effect.

Use spray starch before cutting fabric to add 'body' to a limp, soft or fine material. Stiffer materials usually crease better and support the texture more efficiently.

Thread selection
Experiment with colour, type and thickness. Explore the effect of some of the fabulous variegated threads which are available in many sewing and craft stores. Mix a selection of different threads from bulk nylons and flosses to metallic and other decorative threads. *Remember to check the tensions before you begin (page 11).*

Simple tucked cushion
Combine cream coloured thread and fabric for a lightly textured panel. Attach a border and a back and   ....   Hey Presto! A cushion.

For a 31 cm (12½") panel, you need
One 70 x 30 cm (**28 x 12"**) rectangle
Thread to match fabric
50 cm (**18"**) border and backing
50 cm (**12"**) square wadding/batting
(2 oz low loft polyester or cotton/wool
wadding is useful.)

Drawing by 'Biker' Dave Royce

Serger Settings

Needles: Thread both. (Remove right needle if using three threads - page 10)
Blade: Disengage or set at a maximum distance from needles
Tensions: Regular
Stitch Length: Normal
Stitch width: Reduce to 0.65 cm (¼") by adjusting the stitch finger position (page 12)

1. On the **R**ight **S**ide (R/S) draw small neat and clearly visible marks (use a pencil, chalk or fabric marker) along both long edges at 2.5 cm (**1"**) intervals. Mark one edge first then mark the opposite one - both sets of marks on each edge should be aligned. <u>Do not rule lines across the fabric.</u>

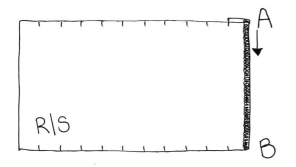

2. Fold fabric on the first set of marks (pencil mark on the edge of fold). Serge from edge to edge. <u>If the blade is still engaged, do not let it cut the fabric - no chunks should be carved from the folded edge.</u> Try to sew a parallel seam to the fold. Chain off at the end of the seam onto a thread saver (page 18). The first tuck is now completed.

Wasn't that really difficult?

3. Turn the work round and refold the fabric on the next set of marks. Serge along the fold making a second tuck.

Repeat the folding and stitching on every set of marks. Turn the work each time, sewing each tuck in the opposite direction to the previous one to prevent the tucked fabric distorting.

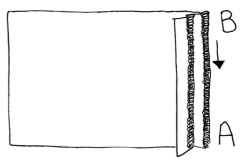

When lines of stitch are constantly sewn in the same direction i.e. top A to bottom B, the presser foot drags the fibres slightly each time, consequently pulling the material out of shape. By commencing sewing from A towards B, turning work and sewing next seam from B to A, the fibres will be less distorted.

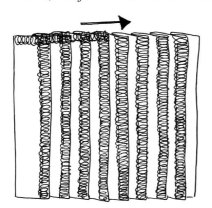

PS. As the work is turned, on every other seam the tucks will be underneath.

4. Continue until all the tucks are made or boredom sets in! Press all the tucks firmly in the same direction; press both the tucked (right) side and the reverse (wrong) side well. Do not worry if the seam lines on the reverse appear to be uneven, as once the tucks have been manipulated any little meanders will be concealed.

5. <u>Increase the stitch length to maximum</u> and serge along one edge of the tucks.

Tip: Turn the fabric so the stitched edges of the tucks are facing you. It is much easier to sew the tucks in the same direction as they were pressed. Go with the flow!

6. Serge the opposite edge of the tucks. <u>Now</u> you have a choice: the tucks can lie in the direction they were pressed or flipped over to create a twist.

Tip: Flip the tucks over with a barbecue skewer (page 18).

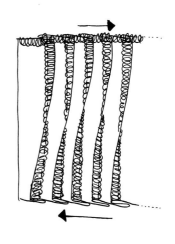

7. Add a border (page 82). Press the border seams towards the outside edge.

8. Lay the completed panel on the square of wadding. Pin in place and serge round the outside edge. Engage the blade and keep the stitch length set at maximum. Set the blade so that it trims the wadding to the raw edge of the panel.

9. Measure the panel and cut another piece of material the same size. Place this backing on the R/S of the panel. Pin carefully keeping the pins away from the presser foot.

Serger Settings

Needles: Thread both. (Remove right needle if using three threads - page 10)
Blade: Engaged
Tensions: Regular
Stitch Length: Normal
Stitch width: Regular

Sew round the raw edges LEAVING A LARGE GAP along one side (the cushion pad will be inserted through this gap). Remember to sew a gentle curve round all four corners.

10. Turn right side out and stuff pad inside (bet you wish you had left a larger space!). Slip stitch the gap by hand.

For those who abhor this really simple method of making a cushion and worry about washing the cushion there are several options:

a. Insert a zip in the back of the cushion.

b. Make the cushion back out of two pieces of fabric. Fasten the two sections with Velcro, buttons or ties. Alternatively cut two large bits of fabric and overlap (similar to the closure on a pillowcase).

c. Stuff a washable pad into the cover. No need to remove before laundering, just wash then spin the entire article very gently - do not spin into total submission! Sling the soggy cushion in the tumble dryer and dry on a gentle heat. Throw it back on the sofa.

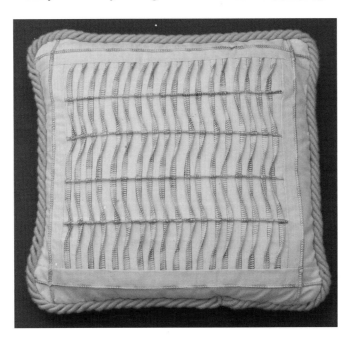

Serged Tuck Cushion

Jennie Rayment

Play a little
Make a panel of tucks. Cut the panel into squares and arrange the sections with the tucks running horizontally and vertically. Sew the squares together. Add a border. (See coloured photographs.)

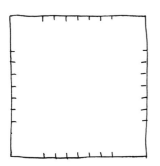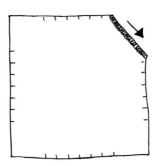

How about tucking the fabric on the bias (diagonal)?
Take a large square of material and mark the sides at 2.5 cm (**1"**) intervals as shown. Fold the fabric on the diagonal and make the tucks as described on page 87. Press the completed tucks in the same direction. Add a border.

For more ornamentation, fold one side of the border in half width-ways and press. Sew a narrow tuck along the pressed edge. (Watch the blade - do not cut bits off the pressed edge.) Make another tuck on the opposite side of the panel before repeating the tuck on the two remaining sides.

Place the panel on some wadding. Pin in place.

Now for a little extra embellishment, add a decorative finish:
Cut twelve 7.5 cm (**3"**) squares. Fold as indicated in the diagram below.

This particular method of folding is usually called a Somerset Patch (UK) or Sharks Tooth (USA).

Pin the folded shapes (R/S down) to the edges of the panel aligning the raw edges.

Serge round the outside edge to anchor all the layers, trimming the excess wadding with the blade.

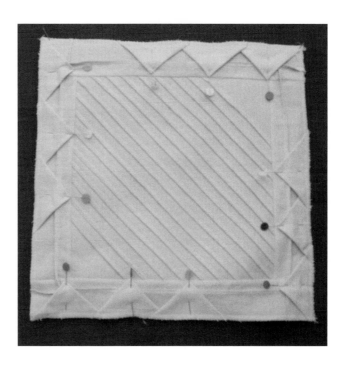

Attach a back and there you are - a neatly chic and pleasantly decorative cushion. (For completed sample see coloured photographs.)

Tuck twisting

Make a panel of tucks as described in Stages 1 - 4 (page 87). Why not use a variegated thread to emphasise the stitching? Follow Stages 3 - 6 (pages 81 - 82) and twist the tucks in opposite directions - just twiddle them over.

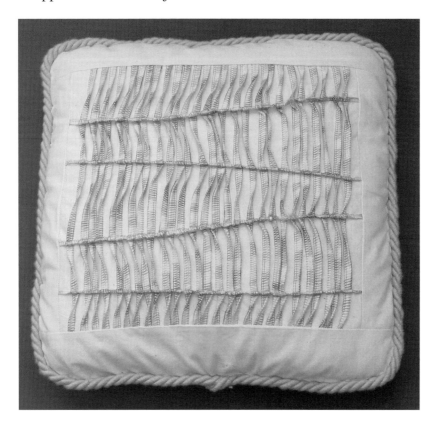

Experiment with twisted tucks

a. Do the tucks have to be twisted at evenly spaced intervals? Change the spacing between the lines.

It is advisable to leave at least 5 - 6 cm (2 - 2½") *between each line of stitching or the fabric may distort.* Alternatively, sew across the panel at an angle, twisting the rows of tucks in opposite directions each time.

b. Mark the fabric on the R/S at 5 cm (**2"**) intervals instead of every 2.5 cm (**1"**). Fold on the marks and make the tucks. Sew across the tucks at the same interval twisting the lines of tucks on opposite directions.

c. Try the same effect on the diagonal.

d. Forget about marking the edge of the material at even intervals. Make the tucks any which way you like. (The outside edges of the panel will need to be trimmed level on completion.)

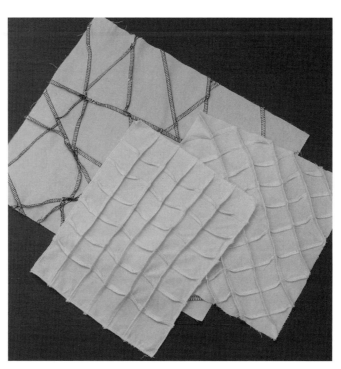

Finally......... Try a little flatlock

Mark all sides of a 30 cm (12½") square at 6 cm (2½") intervals.

1. Thread the serger with a thread which contrasts with the fabric - using a coloured thread that matches the material can obscure the pattern of the flatlock stitch.

Serger Settings: Flatlock

Needles: Remove right-hand needle.
Blade: Disengage
Tensions: Loosen left-hand needle tension - turn to lowest number
　　　　 Tighten lower looper - turn to highest number
Stitch Length: Reduce to smaller stitch length
Stitch width: Widest. Set stitch finger at maximum (page 12).

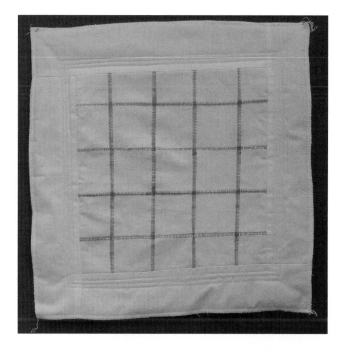

2. Decide which side of the flatlock seam will be uppermost (page 15). Fold the fabric on each set of marks and sew a flatlock seam. Work vertically or horizontally first - the choice is yours. Pull the fabric firmly to flatten the stitching and press well.

3. Repeat in the opposite direction to complete the grid of evenly spaced flatlocking. Pull the fabric firmly to flatten the stitching as in Stage 2. Press well.

Play on. .... Combine random serged tucks and flatlock seams for an intriguing textural abstract design.

1. Cut a large piece of fabric. No need to cut an exact square or strip, as the completed panel has to be trimmed.

2. Fold the fabric R/S out in any direction. Flatlock along the fold. Repeat in a different direction. Continue working on this side of the material, folding at intermittent intervals. Turn the fabric W/S out and repeat the random flatlocking on this side. Using both sides of the material in this fashion will ensure that both different stitch patterns of the flatlock will be visible on the completed work (page 15).

3. Firmly pull all the seams flat and press the material well.

4. Reset the serger to regular sewing. To optimise the three-dimensional textured effect (good phrase!) change the thread to match the colour of the material. Sometimes a certain amount of textural definition is lost when the tucks are formed with coloured thread.

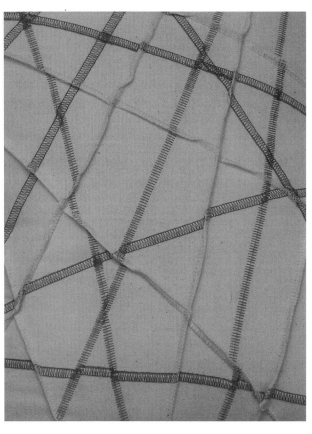

5. Fold the fabric on the R/S and sew some tucks in an abstract formation.

6. Trim the sides of the panel level. Add borders if desired.

Further ideas

Serging the edge of a tuck is most effective, especially when using a thread which contrasts with the fabric. In both '**Tucks & Textures Two**' and '**Creative Tucks and Textures**', there are instructions for tucking up a circle. Why not make the tucks on the serger instead of the sewing machine?

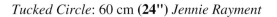

**The potential for play with the serger is extensive so have a go.
Why not?**

Tucked Circle: 60 cm (**24"**) *Jennie Rayment*

Weaving for Wussies

Why the title? I just liked it. What's a wussy? A wussy is an Australian word meaning faint-hearted, lacking in 'get up and go', a real wuss in other words. There are times in life when you just have to put up with things and get on with it - wuss doesn't come into it.

Losing your grip
Two years ago, my dentist tightened the last nut, cemented the last rivet then pronounced my complex and amazingly expensive gnashers complete. A new set of teeth had been bolted into the upper jaw with giant staples or so it seemed but the bottom lot were removable. These needed to be removed each day for cleaning.

I had flown to Chicago on a ten day teaching tour. All keen and eager, I arose early on the first morning, slightly jet-lagged but raring to go. Zipped into the bathroom and had quick shower. Cleaned top set of fangs and hoicked out the bottom lot for a good brushing. Amazing what gets trapped beneath! Odd particles flew out as I merrily wafted the brush back and forth. Holding my teeth in my left hand, I grabbed a tissue and wiped the bits from the sides of the basin (can't leave it dirty for the room-maid!). Dropped tissue down loo and pulled the chain. As I did, my left elbow caught the doorjamb. This caused a reflex action in the muscles of my left hand - they twitched violently. The teeth shot from my hand up in a neat parabola and straight down the still flushing lavatory. Gone!

I had just flushed my highly expensive teeth down the pan. .... This is where the Dunkirk spirit kicks in....... I girded my loins (put some clothes on) and strode down to the lobby. " Excuse me. I wonder if you can help, please. I have just flushed my teeth down the loo. Could you ask the janitor to see if he can find them." I had hoped there might be some form of sewage trap. I didn't mind what they were muddled up in - the teeth would wash!

No, they had gone down through the drains and were out in the lake. Probably some huge fish is now sporting a fantastic set of lower teeth and is looking for the top lot.

It was not that hard managing for ten days without teeth. A diet of cereal and soup is almost acceptable but the big problem was my speech. The letter 'S' was impossible. When you teach stitching and sewing and you can only say 'thtitching' and 'thewing' then people do wonder what you have been imbibing.

THE FISH FELT VERY BEAUTIFUL WITH HER NEW TEETH

Weaving for Wussies

This chapter covers two different methods for creating woven designs. Weaving with stiffened and stitched strips is the first. This is a most excellent technique for creating attractive heat resistant tablemats. The second method involves weaving with a wiggle. Wiggly Weaving is suitable for cushions, bags, garments and quilt blocks in addition to tablemats. Very little sewing is involved in the initial construction - an added bonus!

Both designs are can be completed on any 3 - 4 thread overlockers, although 'Wiggly Weaving' could be embellished with a simple decorative stitch on a cover stitch serger or a basic swing needle sewing machine.

Play with contrasting coloured fabrics in a variety of patterns. Stripes and most geometric forms will produce some interesting visual effects BUT, if you are very pernickety, cut the fabric carefully. Wibbly wobbly weaving lines might make you woeful!

Woven tablemats. Shopping bag, cushion, table mats and card featuring Wiggly Weaving. Jennie Rayment

Weaving with Stiffened Strips

This technique makes the most splendid reversible heat resistant table mats. Why not make a set of mats to co-ordinate with your favourite table linen or will suit a festive occasion?

Fabric choice
Select two contrasting coloured plain or lightly patterned medium-weight cottons or silks. It is advisable to pre-wash before use, and when pressing use spray starch or a similar preparation to restore the 'body' to the washed material.

Thread selection
In my opinion, using only three threads as opposed to four on the serger is the better option (page 10). Select a good quality floss or bulk (woolly) nylon thread for use on the upper and lower loopers in colours that compliment the fabrics. Use an ordinary regular-weight polyester or cotton thread through the needle.

For one 20 cm (7½") square mat: you need
Four 21 x 22 cm (**8 x 8½"**) rectangles - fabric in two contrasting colours
Two 21 x 22 cm (**8 x 8½"**) rectangles - regular weight fusible interfacing (page 16/17)
Thread to match or contrast materials

> ***P.S. Instead of always saying 'fusible interfacing' in this chapter, sometimes I have shortened it to read 'interfacing' - it is still the same stuff. (Saves typing the word fusible so much!)***

1. Select two 21 x 22 cm (**8 x 8½"**) rectangles of the same coloured fabric. Fuse one rectangle to each side of one fusible interfacing section. Fuse the remaining two rectangles of material to the other piece of interfacing.

Tip: Place a piece of waxed/greaseproof paper or a non-stick pressing sheet directly under the iron to prevent any surplus glue from the fusible interfacing edge adhering to the iron (page 17).

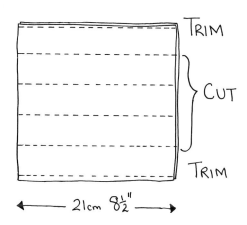

2. Take one of the fabric covered sections of fusible interfacing. Trim one 22 cm (**8½"**) side to ensure the fabric and the interfacing are level. Cut the remainder into five 4 x 22 cm (**1½ x 8½"**) strips. Use a rotary cutter and ruler or draw lines at 4 cm (**1½"**) intervals across the rectangle and cut through the lines with scissors.

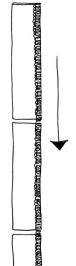

3. Test the machine stitching on a spare scrap of fabric and fusible interfacing. If the thread tensions are not correct now is the time to adjust the settings.

Serger Settings

Needles: Remove right-hand needle - thread left-hand needle only
Blade: Engaged
Tensions: Regular
Stitch Length: Normal
Stitch width: Narrow - retract stitch finger (page 12)

4. Sew one long side of all the strips aligning the edge of the strip with the edge of the presser foot. The blade should trim the odd few whiskers from the fabric not remove great chunks from the edge.

Tip: Save thread by sewing directly onto the next strip without chaining off. Butt the strips together as you feed them under the presser foot, and leave the threads connected.

5. Turn the strip round and sew the other long side. Be careful to sew with the same side of the strip upward to keep the stitch pattern the same. On completion of all the sewing, cut the threads between the strips.

6. Weave the strips together - one colour runs horizontally, the other vertically.

Tip: Lay the pieces on a ruled cutting mat or any other surface with a grid-like pattern. Align the strips with the straight lines of the mat or grid.

Make sure the sets of strips are at right-angles to each other - in other words - wriggle all the pieces into nice straight parallel lines. Remove any gaps between the sections.

Hold the strips in place by stabbing pins through the two layers like spears, as opposed to pushing the pin in and out of both layers in the usual fashion. Pushing pins through two layers of fusible interfacing is hard work and some pins may bend. (Long rigid pins with bright yellow heads usually known as'Quilters Pins' are ideal for this task.)

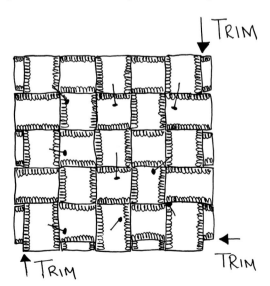

7. Trim the ends of the fusible interfacing level with the sides of the mat. With a bit of luck, the mat is now square and should measure 20 cm (7½") approximately. Leave the pins in place - watch you don't stab yourself with the sharp ends.

Tip: Spitting on any blood and then rubbing with white cotton thread removes most stains. As a copious quantity of spit is better than a mere dribble, suggest this be done away from the public gaze. :o)

8. The woven strips are held together with a solid line of overlocking/serging round the outside edge.

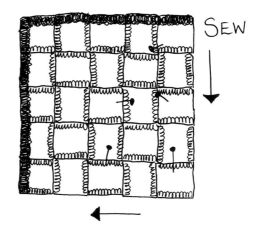

Increase the stitch width to maximum (replace stitch finger). Sew carefully round the sides of the woven square. For successful turning of the corners follow Pam Neave's advice on page 14.

9. Tie off any loose threads (page 13).

The completed mat is not only heat-resistant but double sided. How advantageous - less washing! When the mat gets really grubby on one side, turn it over and use the other. Much more environmentally friendly!

Now washing reminds me of why teeth-cleaning in an automatic 'hole in the wall' hand washing machines is definitely not advisable. I was in a Macdonald's - why? They have a loo/restroom/washroom and open early. An ideal venue for a quick pit stop after a long journey to tidy up, wash hands and generally get ready for teaching or lecturing. On this occasion, I just needed to clean teeth. Armed with toothbrush, I pressed the start button on the 'AutoMac Wash' basin. An unappetising splodge of pink goo landed on my brush - soap! I had pre-empted the machine - should have waited for the water. Flicking the soap off the brush I applied the toothpaste. A moment later, the water arrived so I tried to get my head over the basin - difficult. AutoMacWash basins were not designed for your head consequently I dribbled down the side of the bowl. The water stopped and suddenly.......hot air issued forth at such a rate that it blew the toothpasty dribble out from the basin and all over my navy blue shirt.

Moral of this story: ....Stop in a motorway service station - they have decent sized hand basins, enough room for performing all normal sorts of ablutions and usually proper taps.

But...............Take a little care ....In some public washrooms, the taps are sensor-activated, and leaving your bag in the adjacent basin may cause a problem. I did just that, and as I endeavoured to apply mascara someone tapped me on the shoulder and said "Mam, your purse is filling up with water!"

More ideas with this technique
a. Experiment with different types and colours of thread, both for sewing down the long sides of the strips and for the final stitching round the mat.

b. Replace the fusible interfacing with a lighter-weight interfacing. This will make the mats more pliable BUT less heat-resistant.

c. Cut the strips in a variety of widths from a selection of fabrics. Why use just two colours? Every piece could be a different colour.

Wiggly Weaving

Two pieces of material are required for this simple technique. Both fabrics are bonded to a fabric glue web such as Bondaweb or Trans-web, then cut into pieces with a wiggly line, woven and bonded in place. Each completed panel is subtly unique - no two randomly curved cuts will be exactly the same.

Wiggly Weaving can be incorporated in quilts, garments, bags and cushions. It even makes an unusual table mat. Embellish, enhance and embroider or leave the weaving elegantly plain, the choices is yours.

Fabric choice

Select two contrasting coloured plain or lightly patterned medium-weight cottons or silks. Batiks, glazed cottons/chintz and other firmly woven materials are an excellent choice because they do not stretch when the adhesive is ironed on. Pre-washing the fabrics is advisable (be aware that glazed cottons often lose their sheen when laundered). Spray the washed material lightly with a starch or similar stiffening preparation to restore the 'body'.

For one 25 cm (10") square panel: you need
Two 25 x 28 cm **(10 x 11")** rectangles of fabric in two contrasting colours
Two 25 x 28 cm **(10 x 11")** rectangles of any fabric glue web (Bondaweb, Trans-web or similar product)
One 28 cm **(11")** square of light or medium weight sew-in interfacing
Two 31 cm **(12")** sheets of waxed/greaseproof paper or two pressing sheets to protect the iron and ironing board from glue damage (page 17).
Padded surface such as an old towel or well padded ironing board cover

Wiggly Weaving cushion
Jennie Rayment

1. Fuse one 25 x 28 cm **(10 x 11")** fabric glue web to the W/S of each fabric rectangle. Remember: Sandwich the fabric and the glue web between the waxed paper or pressing sheets.

Tip: Check the recommended temperature required for fusing the glue web to the fabric - read the instructions!

2. Lay both rectangles of fabric together (R/Ss up).

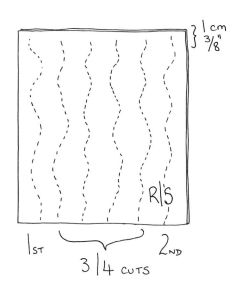

3. Using either scissors or a rotary cutter; cut a randomly curved line through both materials. Make the cut along the 28 cm **(11")** length. Keep outer edge of the random curve at least 1.5 cm **(½")** from raw side of the fabrics. **STOP** cutting approximately 1 cm **(³/₈")** from the end of the material.

4. Cut another curved line on the opposite side of the material. Make the second cut a different curve to the first one. **STOP** cutting approximately 1 cm **(³/₈")** from the end of material.

5. Make three or four more random cuts through both pieces of material. **STOP** cutting approximately 1 cm **(³/₈")** from the end of material each time.

Leaving a small uncut section of fabric holds the cut strips together. Cutting right through all the material separates the strips. Getting them back in the right order can be time-consuming.

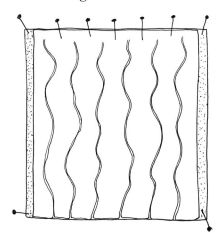

6. Separate the two pieces of material.

7. Put the 28 cm **(11")** square of interfacing on the padded surface. Secure each of the corners with a pin. Lay one of the cut rectangles of fabric on top (R/S up) as shown in the diagram. Arrange the rectangle on the interfacing with a 1.25 cm **(½")** gap on either side of the fabric. Push pins through the uncut edge of the fabric into the padded surface. These pins hold the fabric steady when you weave.

8. Place the second rectangle of material at right angles to the first rectangle. Leave a 1.25 cm **(½")** gap on either side of the fabric. Pin the uncut edge into the padded surface as described above.

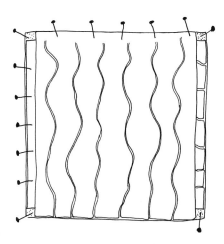

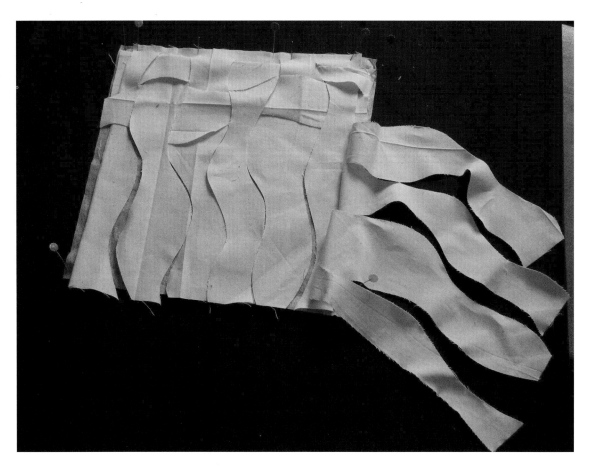

Wiggly Weaving ready to be woven!

9. Weave the cut strips together. Wiggle the strips into place; the strips will fit together exactly - they were cut from the same piece of fabric. Take care to match the intersections of the weaving accurately. Secure the ends of each strip with pins pushed into the padded surface

10. On completion of the weaving, press the panel well and remove the pins. *Remember the waxed paper/pressing sheet between the top of the fabric and the iron.*

11. Turn the panel to the W/S and press the layers firmly to ensure that all strips are firmly bonded in place. The fusible web on the back of the material glues the cut strips both to each other and to the interfacing.

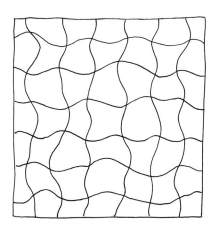

12. Trim the excess interfacing and trim off the uncut sections of the rectangles to form a 25 cm (**10"**) square.

Add embellishment *(This section is optional)*
Decorate the edges of the woven strips with a fancy stitch pattern on the sewing machine or a cover stitch serger. Thread machine top and bottom with a contrasting or complimentary colour to the selected materials and sew over the raw edges of the strips. Choose a pattern with a wide stitch width but not too elaborate. (Very intricate patterns take for ever to sew and are horrendous to unpick.) Align the centre of the presser foot with the raw edge of the strip. Sew over all the raw edges of all the strips.

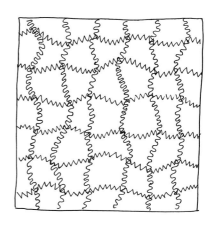

Use the recommended presser foot (see instruction book) for the selected pattern.

For a little extra ornamentation couch a decorative yarn/embroidery silk or similar fibre over the strips. Set a wide stitch width; thread with invisible/nylon filament and zigzag over the yarn (coloured photographs).

Add a border
Two easy methods to border the 25 cm (**10"**) panel. (Regular settings on the serger.)

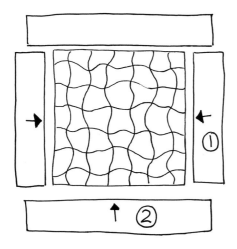

a. Strips
1. Decide on the width of the border e.g. 8 cm (**3"**). Cut two strips this width x 25 cm (**10"**) in length. Attach one strip to the opposite sides of the woven panel.

2. Measure the new width of the panel - it will be approximately 37 cm (**14"**) and cut two more strips this length by 8 cm (**3"**) in width.

3. Attach these strips to the remaining sides. Press well.

b. Triangles - set panel on point
1. Cut two 19 cm (**7½"**) squares. Divide diagonally.

2. Sew one triangle to either side of the panel.

3. Open out and attach the last two triangles to the remaining sides. Press well.

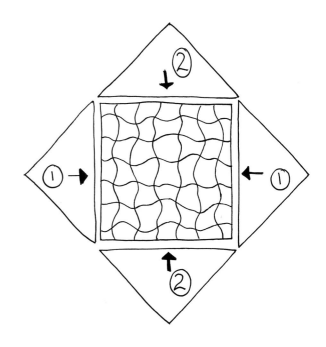

Make a Wiggly Woven cushion

Pin the bordered panel on a piece of wadding/batting. Serge the outside edge to anchor the fabric to the wadding. Add a backing and ....Viola.... A cushion.

To digress..............If you read page 39 you would be aware that French is not my best subject. Nor it would seem is spelling. Wanting to add a cosmopolitan flavour to my prose, I added a few foreign words. Sent some proofs to my father to correct. He enquired politely if I meant the musical instrument or did I really mean the French expression 'Voilà'. Just as well I don't teach spelling or the consequences might be viol!

More ideas

a. Miniaturise the technique for cards: Make a large panel of finely cut strips then cut into several smaller sections. Create several cards at the same time.

b. Heat-resistant tablemats: Bond the cut strips directly to some form of craft-weight interfacing. Fuse a plain piece of material to the back. Serge round the edge and 'Bingo' ....A mat!

Tip: Cut the corners of the mat in a gentle arc (curves are easier to sew than corners).

c. Why not cut the Wiggly Weaving panel into a circle? Simply put a plate or any round object on top of the fabric, draw round and cut on the line. Ideal for round table mats.

Play with the technique, experiment with colour, and try directional fabrics. Wiggly Weaving with stripes could be sensational. How about combining two shades of aquamarine for the background to a seascape or underwater scene? Appliqué boats, fish, mermaids or indeed mermen on top.

Finally, 'Wiggly Weaving' hides a multitude of sins for all those who can't sew straight. Why wobble when you can wiggle?

Remember 'Mistakes do not matter - it is just a little different' and who wants to be the same as anyone else?

Triangle and Hexagon Templates

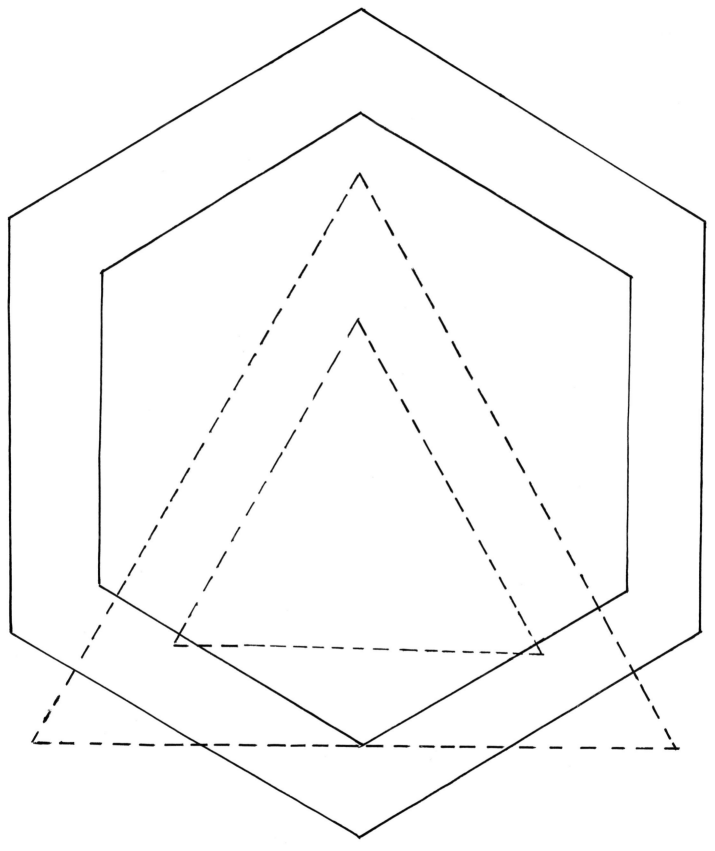

To increase or decrease size of templates:
1. **Use the photocopier.** (Be careful if photocopying templates, check that they are exact replicas, not all copiers are reproduce accurately.)
2. **Trace template. Draw lines inside or outside the template parallel to the sides of the selected shape.**

Glossary

Backing: The fabric used underneath a sample or the underside of a cushion or quilt.
Baste: Securing of layers with a long stitch to prevent movement.
Batting: See Wadding.
Bias: Diagonal grain-line of the material (45°).
Bondaweb/Wundaweb/Heat 'n Bond: Fusible glue web used for sticking fabrics together.
Calico: (UK) Plain woven strong cotton cloth (sometimes bleached) from natural thread.
Catch: Several small stitches in the same place for securing an edge/corner of material.
Chintz: Close-weave shiny cotton cloth with a resin coating for that characteristic sheen.
Cretonne: A washable hard-wearing fabric similar to unglazed chintz; liable to shrink.
Darning Foot: Used for freehand embroidery and quilting. Used with feed dogs down/covered and stitch width and length settings to zero.
French Knots: Raised hand embroidery stitch.
Grain: Direction of the weave. Weft fibres run across selvedge to selvedge; warp fibres are parallel to selvedge. Bias grain diagonal at 45° to selvedge.
Hopper Foot: See Darning foot.
Interfacing: Bonded fibre fabric used as underlay or stiffening material. Made in several thicknesses.
Loft: Amount a wadding/batting rises on quilting.
Log Cabin Patchwork: Traditional designs made from strips of material frequently laid out in a square format. The square is often divided diagonally into light and dark colours.
Mercerised Cotton: Treated both to strengthen and to have a silky sheen.
Muslin: : (UK) Fine soft open weave cotton fabric.
Pellon: Interfacing/stabiliser made from bonded fibres, in different thickness (**USA trade name**).
Pinwheel: Rotation of one shape at 90° round a central point.
Prairie Points: Squares folded diagonally into quarter triangles.
R/S: Right side of material.
Ruche/Ruching: Gathered material often in a strip, used for decorative effect.
Satin Stitch: The stitch effect produced by increasing the stitch width and decreasing the stitch length of the zigzag stitch on the sewing machine.
S/A or Seam Allowance: Distance between the stitch line and the edge of the fabric.
Selvedge/selvage: The firm edges of the fabric running parallel to the warp threads.
Somerset/Folded Squares: Squares folded in rectangles then in triangles (USA **Sharks Tooth**).
Stabiliser: See Interfacing/Pellon/Vilene
Stay Stitching: Securing of layers with a long stitch to prevent movement.

Tack: (UK) Stablising layers with long stitch USA: small securing stitch in one place.)
Vilene: Interfacing/stabiliser made from bonded fibres, comes in different thickness (**UK trade name**).
W/S: Wrong or underside of fabric.
Wadding: Batting or filling frequently made from polyester or cotton fibres. Used in between or underneath fabric for quilting purposes.

Index

For Workshops and Lectures contact:
Jennie Rayment
5 Queen Street, Emsworth,
Hampshire, PO10 7BJ United Kingdom
+ 44 (0) 1243 374860
e-mail: jenrayment@aol.com
www: jennierayment.com